CULTURES OF THE WORLD®

NORWAY

Sakina Kagda & Barbara Cooke

MARSHALL CAVENDISH BENCHMARK

NEW YORK

PICTURE CREDITS
Cover photo: © David Bartruff / Danita Delimont Stock Photography
AFP: 42 • Age fotostock / Doug Scott: 112 • alt.TYPE / Reuters: 61 • Bes Stock Photo Library: 1, 22, 46, 56, 58, 59, 64, 72, 97, 106, 128 • Bjorn Klingwall: 95 • Camera Press: 44, 67, 99, 100, 108, 115 • David Simson: 89 • Elizabeth Su-Dale: 120, 121 • Focus Team: 3, 4, 26, 65, 66, 68, 74, 123, 124 • HBL Network: 6, 9, 15, 36, 38, 39, 40, 82, 107, 116 • Hulton Deutsch: 28, 29, 32, 34, 35, 88, 101, 113 • Hutchison: 73, 76, 91, 105 • International Photobank: 20, 31, 47, 49, 51, 54, 81, 90, 96 • Johan Berge: 8, 11, 12, 13, 16, 18, 21, 23, 71, 75, 78, 79, 92, 96, 98, 110, 118, 119, 126 • Life File: 7, 111 • Marka / Raffaele Meucci: 3 • Photobank / Photolibrary: 10, 37, 80, 102, 104 • Sonja Henie Center: 109 • Stockfood / Innerhofer Photodes: 122 • The Image Bank: 14, 17, 19, 27, 48, 50, 52, 53, 55, 83, 84

PRECEDING PAGE
Norwegian youth in traditional clothing.

Editorial Director (U.S.): Michelle Bisson
Editors: Deborah Grahame, Mabelle Yeo, June Low
Copyreader: Daphne Hougham
Designer: Jailani Basari
Cover picture researcher: Connie Gardner
Picture researchers: Thomas Khoo, Joshua Ang

Marshall Cavendish Benchmark
99 White Plains Road
Tarrytown, NY 10591
Web site: www.marshallcavendish.us

© Times Editions Private Limited 1995
© Marshall Cavendish International (Asia) Private Limited 2006
All rights reserved. First edition 1995. Second edition 2006.
® "Cultures of the World" is a registered trademark of Times Publishing Limited.

Originated and designed by Times Editions
An imprint of Marshall Cavendish International (Asia) Private Limited
A member of Times Publishing Limited

All Internet sites were correct and accurate at the time of printing. All monetary figures in this publication are in U.S. dollars.

Library of Congress Cataloging-in-Publication Data
Kagda, Sakina, 1939–
    Norway / by Sakina Kagda and Barbara Cooke.— 2nd ed.
        p. cm. — (Cultures of the world)
    Includes bibliographical references and index.
    Summary: "Provides comprehensive information on the geography, history, governmental structure, economy, cultural
        diversity, peoples, religion, and culture of Norway" — Provided by publisher.
        ISBN-13: 978-0-7614-2067-5
        ISBN-10: 0-7614-2067-3
    1. Norway—Juvenile literature. I. Title. II. Series.
    DL409.K34 2006
    948.1—dc22   2005035850

Printed in China

9 8 7 6 5 4 3 2 1

CONTENTS

INTRODUCTION   5

GEOGRAPHY   7
*Mountains • Regions • Climate • New territories
• The Lofoten archipelago • Major cities • Fauna and flora*

HISTORY   23
*The earliest farmers • The Vikings • One Norway • Age of
Greatness • Under Swedish rule • The Kalmar Union • Back to
Sweden • Independent Norway • World War II • Postwar period*

GOVERNMENT   37
*The monarchy • The role of the royal family • Administrative
divisions • The Storting • The cabinet • Political parties
• International cooperation • EU Membership*

ECONOMY   47
*Oil and energy • Manufacturing • Agriculture and forestry
• Fishing • Shipping • Transportation*

ENVIRONMENT   57
*Pollution • Recycling • Polar region • Marine life
• Protected land • Cultural heritage*

NORWEGIANS   65
*Norwegians • Norwegian Finns • The Sami • The role
of women • Norwegian newcomers*

LIFESTYLE   73
*Work • A welfare nation • Health • Birth and baptism
• Confirmation • Education • Houses and gardens*

Many people have a pre-
conceived notion that all
Scandinavians are tall
and blond.

RELIGION   83
The Church of Norway • Old Norse gods • Norway's conversion to Christianity • Other Christian churches • Other religions

LANGUAGE   91
Norwegian • Runic writing • The Sami language

ARTS   97
Sculpture • Painting • Music • Literature • Drama • Movies • Stavkirker *architecture*

LEISURE   107
A nation of skiers • Ice skating • Women in sports • No fences • Explorers

FESTIVALS   117
Constitution Day • Children's Day • Russ *celebrations • Easter • Midsummer's Day • Christmas*

FOOD   123
Smørgåsbord • Typical dishes • Mushroom and berry picking • Cheese, anyone? • "Freia!" • Beer and wine • Coffee • Aquavit—the national drink

MAP OF NORWAY   132

ABOUT THE ECONOMY   135

ABOUT THE CULTURE   137

TIME LINE   138

GLOSSARY   140

FURTHER INFORMATION   141

BIBLIOGRAPHY   142

INDEX   142

Norwegian children find convenient resting spots at the Vigeland Park of sculptures.

INTRODUCTION

CELEBRATING ITS 100 YEARS of independence in 2005, Norway is a relatively young nation with a rich history and enduring traditions. It is a land of majestic mountains, breathtaking fjords, and snow covered plateaus whose people love the great outdoors. Almost half of Norway lies north of the Arctic Circle. The North Cape, located on Norway's Magerøya Island, is the northernmost point in Europe.

Norway is consistently ranked the most livable country in the world, according to the United Nations (UN) Human Development Index. Norwegians care deeply about issues such as human rights, civil rights, and equality of the sexes. They have a strong sense of national identity and wish to retain their independence, even as European borders are disappearing. At the same time, Norwegians remain very much engaged in international affairs and committed to actively promoting global peace and the preservation of the environment. Entering the 21st century, Norwegians keep a balance between tradition and progress.

GEOGRAPHY

NORWAY IS A LONG, narrow country that sits at the top of the European continent. Its total area is 125,017 square miles (323,878 square km). This number does not include Norway's overseas territories, which encompass Svalbard, a group of islands in the Arctic Ocean; Jan Mayen, a volcanic island northwest of Norway; and, in the Antarctic, Bouvet Island, Peter I Island, and Dronning Maud Land, which is a large chunk of the Antarctic Coast between longitudes 45°E and 20°W. Nearly two-thirds of mainland Norway is mountainous. The more than 160,000 lakes and as many islands found in this northern country attest to the ancient glaciers that once scoured its land and coastlines with the movements of tremendous masses of ice, earth, and rock.

Opposite: **Norway still contains many large and small glaciers in its landscape today.**

Below: **A hiker surveys the imposing mountains and serene valley of the Romsdal district in western Norway.**

MOUNTAINS

Norway is one of the most mountainous countries in Europe. Its mountain ranges extend almost the entire length of the country. The glaciers shaped the peaks into such odd forms that they have provoked images of trolls and supernatural spirits. The mountains in the south, which contain the highest peaks in Europe north of the Alps, are called Jotunheimen, or Realm of the Giants.

A few mountains are so steep that no one has ever attempted to scale them. Others have been attempted only in recent years. The 2,000-foot (610-m) Reka in northern Norway has never been climbed. The Troll Wall in Romsdal (western Norway) was first climbed in 1967. Many consider it the most demanding climb in Europe. The retreating glaciers cut some mountains down into *vidder* (VI-der), or mountain plateaus; others were ground down by the weight of the ice sheet, 1.25 miles (2 km) thick, into flat plateaus called *fjell* (fyehl). The most impressive legacy of the glacial erosion in the uplands are the fjords (fyords) of western Norway. These are very deep and narrow inlets of the sea between steep cliffs. The fjords of Norway are sometimes deeper even than the North Sea, although they are often shallower near the coast, where the ice sheet is thinner.

As a mountainous country with a dense river network, most of the power that Norway produces is hydroelectric. Most of its power stations are hydraulic installations located high in mountain regions.

One of the many natural fjords in Norway.

REGIONS

The Norwegians have divided their country into five main regions according to geography and dialects. Vestlandet (West Country), Østlandet (East Country), Sørlandet (South Country), and Trøndelag (Mid-Norway) make up South Norway. Nord-Norge (North Norway) makes up the rest.

In southern Norway, Sørlandet, the smallest region, is located at the southernmost point. The other three main regions of the south are defined by wide mountain barriers. From the southernmost point, a swelling complex of mountain ranges, collectively called Langfjellene, or Long Mountains, runs northward to divide Østlandet from Vestlandet. An eastward sweep of mountains separates the northern edge of Østlandet from Trøndelag. Where the southern half of Norway ends, northern Norway, or Nord-Norge, begins.

VESTLANDET With well-kept villages and coastal towns nestled against a backdrop of majestic mountains, the West Country is the representation of Norway best known to the rest of the world—the picturesque Norway. The ancestors of many Norwegian American immigrants left this area in the 19th century. This narrow coastal zone reaches into the Atlantic Ocean and has many islands and steep-walled narrow fjords cutting deep into the interior mountain region. The major exception is the Jæren Dalane (Plain), south of the city of Stavanger, which has the highest agricultural yields in Norway due to its rich soils, very mild winters, long growing season, and abundant rainfall.

Fishing in the Oslofjord in the southeastern part of Norway.

SØRLANDET Centered around the city of Kristiansand, this southern area has an idyllic coastline that has become Norway's foremost summer vacation area. The land is hilly, but the agricultural season is slightly longer than in Oslo, Norway's capital. The interior of Sørlandet, with its narrow valleys running up into the beginnings of Langfjellene, is very sparsely populated. The people of the scattered settlements there depend on dairy farming, sheep raising, and forestry.

ØSTLANDET The East Country boasts more than half of Norway's population, who live mainly in and around the metropolis of Oslo and in the region around Oslofjord. Although this area is mostly urban and industrial, there is also agriculture, which is found mainly in the lowlands extending eastward and southward toward the Swedish border. The lowlands are intensively cultivated due to favorable conditions such as sufficient rain, the highest summer temperatures in Norway, and rich soil.

The harbor at Risør, one of several towns along the southeastern coast of Norway. This harbor was once a regular port of call for trading ships. Today it is popular with tourists and artists. Its attractions include well-preserved wooden architecture of 1865–1900, the Wooden Boat Festival, and the Chamber Music Festival.

The largest forests in Norway are found between the Swedish border and the Glåma River, east of Oslo. The coastline facing Denmark across the Skagerrak passage, stretching from Oslofjord to the southern tip of Norway, is densely populated and crowded with small towns, villages, and small farms.

About half of Østlandet is forested. The region has a little more than half of Norway's total forest resources and a similar share of the country's total area of fully cultivated land. Østlandet also accounts for more than half of the nation's total production value and trade in the mining and manufacturing industries. These large contributory shares of the national wealth, combined with the concentration of economic activity around Oslofjord, secure for Østlandet the highest average household income in Norway.

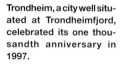

Trondheim, a city well situated at Trondheimfjord, celebrated its one thousandth anniversary in 1997.

TRØNDELAG Mid-Norway, also known as the Trondheim region, is centered around the long Trondheimfjord. Trondheim, the region's major city, is the third largest in Norway. Trøndelag has less industrial development than Østlandet and Vestlandet because there are few suitable sites for power stations. On the eastern shore of the fjord is a small agricultural area.

NORD-NORGE Mountains with jagged peaks and ridges fill most of this region, even the many islands. A long string of large islands jutting into the Atlantic west of Vestfjorden form the Lofoten archipelago. Numerous fjords scissor into this narrow strip of Norway's northern tail. Northern Norway has one of the most irregular coastlines in the world, even more irregular than in the southwest. Nord-Norge has a rugged frontier quality about it, fitting for life in the far north.

Nord-Norge has been called the "the weather kitchen of Europe." Rain, clouds, mist, and fog are characteristic of much of the Norwegian coast, but gales and squalls add a special quality to the north, which has recorded some of the highest wind speeds in the world. Norway's first meteorological station was established there in 1866. As is often said in Nord-Norge, there is a lot of weather to watch.

A harbor in Vesterålen, an archipelago north of the Lofoten islands. From October to February Vesterålen is overrun by the participants in killer whale safaris.

The Norwegian poet Nordahl Grieg (1902–43) said of Nord-Norge in 1922: "This is the real Norway: freezingly sparse and beautiful."

Winter days are longer the farther north one goes in Norway.

CLIMATE

Without the warm waters of the Gulf Stream, which keep the fjords from freezing, Norway's coastal areas would not enjoy temperate and mild climate year round. Even beyond the North Cape, which is farther north than both Siberia and the continent of North America, there are many green forests, and, on sunny days, the beaches are strewed with numerous sunbathers.

Average temperatures for the southern part of Norway near Oslo and Bergen range from freezing in winter to 61°F (16°C) in summer. In northern Norway, the average winter temperature is 23°F (-5°C), and the average summer temperature is about 50°F (10°C), although temperatures have been known to reach as high as 77–86°F (25–30°C).

Norway lies directly in the path of the North Atlantic cyclones, which bring strong winds and frequent changes in weather. Western Norway experiences comparatively cool summers, mild winters, and a substantial amount of rain. Eastern Norway, sheltered by the mountains in the center of the country, experiences warm summers, cold winters, and very little rain.

LAND OF THE MIDNIGHT SUN

The duration of daylight and night varies from one place to another due to the tilt of the earth's axis and the season of the year. At the equator there is hardly any noticeable difference between the number of hours of daylight and the number of hours of darkness, and between summer and winter. The farther north or south one goes, however, the greater is this variation. Located as far north as it is, Norway experiences great variations in seasons and in hours of daylight and night.

In the northern half of Norway, the sun does not set all summer. The area from the Arctic Circle to the North Cape is called the Land of the Midnight Sun, and attracts thousands of tourists. The length of time the sun stays above the horizon declines as one goes south, but the sun never sets on Midsummer's Day (June 23) in all places north of the Arctic Circle.

Even south of the Arctic Circle, summer nights are so bright that people can read their newspapers by natural light in the middle of the night. It is not unusual for Norwegians to take a walk or visit friends at 2 A.M. Norwegians say they have two days for every summer day: one for work and one for *hverdagslivet* (vehr-DAHGS-leev-uht) or daily life.

To make up for all that daylight during summer, those who live north of the Arctic Circle will not see the sun for weeks in winter, although there usually is some daylight around midday.

The Arctic Circle Center is a popular tourist spot. It is situated 1,970 feet (600 m) above sea level in the Saltfjellet National Park.

NEW TERRITORIES

In the late 19th century Fridtjof Nansen's polar expedition came within 272 miles (438 km) of the North Pole. Less than two decades later, Roald Amundsen's expedition was the first to reach the South Pole. Norwegian exploration in polar regions brought new territories under Norway's sovereignty in the 20th century: Svalbard in 1925, Bouvet Island in 1928, Jan Mayen Island in 1929, Peter I Island in 1931, and Dronning Maud Land in 1939.

SVALBARD This archipelago located in the Arctic, 352 miles (567 km) from the northernmost point of mainland Norway, consists of four large islands and a number of small ones covering an area of 38,5572 square miles (998,627 square km). The largest of the islands, Spitsbergen, accounts for more than half of the archipelago's total land area. The landscape is characterized by steep mountains and deep fjords, and vast areas are covered by glaciers. Coal mining constitutes the main mining activity. Svalbard's population of around 2,700 people is concentrated at Longyearbyen, Ny-Ålesund, Barentsburg, and Pyramiden.

ANTARCTIC ISLANDS Norway's three territories in the Antarctic are Bouvet Island, Peter I Island, and Dronning Maud Land. Norway was one of 12 countries that signed the Antarctic Treaty in 1959. In 1991 these countries agreed to maintain the Antarctic as a nature reserve devoted to peace, research, and environmental cooperation. Mineral extraction activity in the area is prohibited for 50 years from 1991.

THE LOFOTEN ARCHIPELAGO

The mountains on various Lofoten islands are sometimes referred to as the Lofoten Wall, perhaps because its islands form a barrier between the northwestern coast of Norway and the Atlantic Ocean. The total area of the Lofoten islands is 475 square miles (1,230 square km), and the principal islands are Austvågøy, Vestvågøy, and Moskenesøy. The Lofoten islands are famous for their fisheries. Commercial anglers crowd the fishing villages on the islands during the cod season, from January to April. The Norwegian Fishing Village Museum and the Dried Fish Museum are both located at Lofoten.

Reine, on the eastern coast of Moskenesøy, is situated in a calm bay.

Dockside houses, seen from a ship in Bergen's harbor. These houses were included in UNESCO's World Heritage list in 1980.

MAJOR CITIES

Norway's three major cities are Oslo, the capital and home to about 530,000 people; Bergen, with a population of almost 240,000; and Trondheim, which ranks third with 157,000 people.

OSLO Norway's capital, situated at the head of the Oslofjord, is the country's main hub for communications, trade, education, research, industry, and transportation. It is also Norway's political and financial heart, and its center for international shipping. Oslo was founded by King Harald III around 1050, but only became the capital of Norway in the 14th century. Destroyed by fire in 1624 and rebuilt as Christiania, it was renamed Oslo in 1924.

BERGEN The natural center of Vestlandet, Bergen has a more international character than any other city in Norway. Since the Middle Ages, it was an active trading center of northern Europe. It was officially founded in 1070 by King Olav III, "The Peaceful" (ruled 1069–93). Unlike Trondheim and Oslo, Bergen has no fertile land. It lies amid seven mountains facing the sea. Said to have been a starting point for many Viking seafaring expeditions, Bergen grew as a fishing and trading port.

Present-day Bergen is the second-largest city in Norway and is still the principal port on the west coast, with a considerable merchant fleet, several large shipyards, and one of Norway's six universities.

TRONDHEIM Trondheim, in Trøndelag, is Norway's historic capital. It was founded in 997 by Viking king Olav Tryggvason (ruled 995–1000). In the Middle Ages, Trondheim was an important commercial, administrative, and religious core. Norway's first abbey was built on an island outside the city, and Nidaros Cathedral, an important pilgrimage site, is also there.

Trondheim, Norway's technology capital, has been a research center since as early as 1760, when Norway's Royal Scientific Society founded a museum and research station in the city. Norway's first seat of learning is a school founded by the Nidaros Cathedral monks. In 1900 the technical school was transformed into a college, known today as the Norwegian Institute of Technology. SINTEF (The Foundation for Scientific and Industrial Research) at the Norwegian Institute of Technology is a state-funded research institute that concentrates on marine and information technology in Norway and abroad. The national Ship Research Institute is located there, as well as a biological research station with an aquarium.

OTHER CITIES Apart from being the oil capital of Norway, Stavanger in southwest Norway is the prime area for agricultural research. Tromsø, Norway's largest city north of the Arctic Circle, is home to the world's leading research organization for the Arctic phenomena.

An aerial view of Oslo's waterfront. Oslo's location between mountains and the sea gives its residents many advantages, including skiing in winter and sailing in summer.

19

A herd of mountain goats graze on Hardanger Plateau. The area is famous for goat's milk and cheese.

FAUNA AND FLORA

Reindeer, wolverines, and other Arctic animals live throughout Norway, although in the south they are found only in mountain areas. Elk are found in the forests and red deer on the west coast. Although common as recently as 100 years ago, bear, wolf, wolverine, and lynx are found in only a few areas, mainly in the north. Foxes and otters are common, and badgers and beavers inhabit many areas. The beaver is an example of a successful program of protection. Prior to 1940 the entire European stock of beavers was around 500 to 600, and those beavers were found largely in southern Norway. State protection increased their population to the extent that Norway was able to send beavers to Switzerland, Russia, and the Czech Republic.

A small rodent periodically found in large numbers is the lemming. People speak of a lemming year, when mountainous regions teem with thousands of these small animals, providing predators with a rich food source. The dazzlingly white snowy owl of the North Pole will fly thousands of miles to a good supply of lemmings. How it knows when lemmings are plentiful is one of nature's mysteries.

Nesting cliffs are filled with millions of kittiwakes, puffins, guillemots, auks, cormorants, and gulls. The sea eagle, an endangered species about fifty years ago, is now thriving. Lakes and marshes are inhabited by cranes, whooper swans, grebes, geese, ducks, and other waders.

Along the coast there are large numbers of seals and whales. Most rivers have fish, notably trout and salmon. Large schools of salmon are found in at least 160 rivers, attracting anglers from all over the world.

Norway has about 2,000 species of plants, but only a few, mainly mountain plants, are particular to Norway. Thick forests of spruce and pine thrive in the broad glacial valleys of eastern Norway and in the Trondheim region. In western Norway there are virtually no conifers. North of the Arctic Circle there is little spruce, and pine grows mainly in the inland valleys. The pine, spruce, and other Norwegian conifers, such as juniper and yew, retain their needlelike leaves throughout the year. In winter the needles curl up to retain moisture.

Wild berries grow throughout Norway, including blueberries, cranberries, and cloudberries, a species that belongs to the rose family and is little known outside Scandinavia and the United Kingdom.

Climate is a prime factor in determining the distribution patterns of plant life in Norway. Along the west coast, where winter is mild and snowfalls rare, plants that cannot tolerate frost, such as the star hyacinth and purple heather, thrive. Farther inland grow species that can withstand short periods of frost and snow in the winter: the foxglove and holly are typical plants. Around Oslo, the long, cold winter and dry, warm summer provide the right climate for species like the blue anemone and the aconite.

Norwegians call these blue anemones *blåveis* (BLOW-vays). They are one of numerous species of flowers that appear in the wilderness every summer.

HISTORY

THE EARLIEST TRACES of humans in Norway were found along the coast of Finnmark and north of Stadlandet in the west. Archaeologists believe these humans lived between 9000 B.C. and 8000 B.C., by which time most of the glacial ice had receded. These earliest inhabitants may have migrated from Finland and Russia around 10,000 B.C., when the interior was still covered with ice. Another theory is that they came considerably later from the south and traveled northward.

THE EARLIEST FARMERS

Before 3000 B.C., the inhabitants of Norway lived in tentlike shelters and coastal mountain caves. They hunted and fished. Between 3000 B.C. and 1500 B.C., warlike Germanic tribes migrated to Norway. From them, the earlier inhabitants learned to attach handles to tools to make them more efficient. During this period eastern Norway was settled by other migrants—farmers who grew barley and kept cows and sheep. The hunter-fishers of the west coast were gradually replaced by these farmers, although hunting and fishing remained in use. This gave rise to permanent farming settlements, which were usually situated along the coast and near lakes.

Isolated from each other by mountains and fjords, the farming communities became independent small states with their own leaders. By the eighth century, 30 states existed in Norway. By the ninth century, the states were divided into districts, each with its own assembly, where grievances were settled in accordance with written laws.

Above: **Rock carvings in Nord-Trøndelag tell the stories of early inhabitants.**

Opposite: **The first Mass in Norway was held in the 12th century at Saint Mary's Church in Bergen.**

The lawmaking assemblies—the Gulating in the west, the Frostating in Trøndelag, and the Eidsvating in the east—had come into existence by the year 900.

23

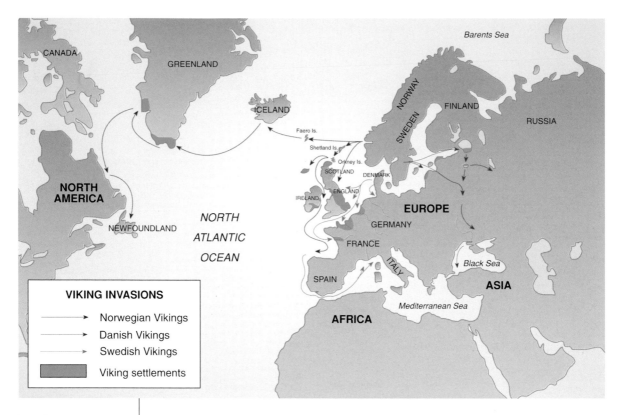

VIKING INVASIONS

→ Norwegian Vikings

→ Danish Vikings

→ Swedish Vikings

▨ Viking settlements

The Swedish Vikings sailed east to Russia and visited Constantinople (Istanbul). The Norwegians and Danes headed west and south toward Europe. The Norwegians primarily headed west, raiding and settling in northern England and Scotland, going south through the Irish Sea to Ireland and down into Wales. Later they traveled to Iceland, Greenland, and North America.

THE VIKINGS

Perhaps the most famous Scandinavians are the Vikings. In the Viking Age (A.D.793–1066), the Scandinavians set out over the oceans to conquer new territories and expand their markets. One theory behind this desire for conquest is that the rapid population growth that seems to have occurred from A.D. 600 led to a shortage of land, prompting many to look overseas for their fortunes. The Vikings came from Norway, Sweden, and Denmark, and each had different routes of conquest and trade.

The Vikings were the only Western sailors in early medieval times who dared to sail beyond landmarks into uncharted waters. They discovered Svalbard, the Arctic islands northwest of Norway. Before A.D.1000 they had settled in all the habitable islands in the North Atlantic, including the Shetlands, the Orkneys, the Faeroe Islands, Iceland, and Greenland, which all remained under Norwegian influence for centuries. They also landed on the shores of North America 500 years before Christopher Columbus did.

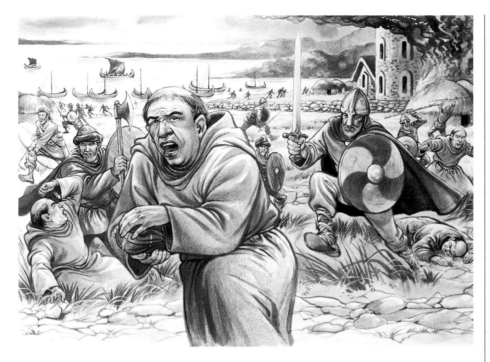

VIOLENT VIKINGS The Vikings had a reputation of being pirates because of their warlike raids on other European communities that characterized the first 100 years of the Viking Age. The earliest recorded raid of the Norwegian Vikings was in 793. Landing quickly and unexpectedly on the island of Lindisfarne, off the northeast coast of England, a small party of raiders looted the monastery, set it on fire, slaughtered many monks, and took others captive. They then sped away in their dragonhead boats, disappearing as quickly as they had appeared. This left the English in a state of shock, for they had not believed such a sea attack possible. This success encouraged the Norwegian Vikings to launch more raids against northern England, Scotland, and Ireland. Monasteries were the first targets because they had wealth and few defenses. These small pirate raids were followed by larger, bolder, and better-organized attacks, sometimes with military expeditions of dozens of ships under a commanding chieftain.

Norwegians themselves see the Viking times as more complex. Many claim that not all Norwegians of that time should be called Vikings, just the warriors. They point out that most Norwegians were farmers and fisherfolk, who quietly went about their daily lives.

This reconstruction of a Viking house shows how the Vikings lived: the house is a single long room with timber walls, a dirt floor, and a roof covered with shingles and grass. Large pieces of stone reinforce the walls. A hole in the roof allows smoke from a hearth to escape. There are no windows, and light enters only through the doorway and slits in the wall, so the room is dark and musty.

CREEKMEN OR WARRIORS?

The origin of the word "Viking" has long been a mystery. Some scholars believe it meant "creekmen," basing this on the Old Norse word *vic*, meaning creek or inlet. Others insist it referred to a pirating center, the Vik, in the Oslofjord. Yet another theory is that the term originated from the Old English word *wic*, meaning warrior.

The Europeans whose lands were invaded by Vikings did not speculate much on the origin of the term and did not differentiate Swedish Vikings from Danish Vikings or Norwegian Vikings. They simply referred to them as "men from the north"—Norsemen or Northmen. A popular prayer in the ninth century was, "From the fury of the Northmen, deliver us, O Lord." The early Vikings themselves identified with their local districts, calling themselves "men of Hardanger" or "men of Vestfold." Only toward the end of the Viking age did a concept of national identity begin to develop.

VIKING LIFE Historians tell us that many Viking settlements were based on trade, were well organized, and had a high level of architecture and artistry. They had law assemblies that convened once a year to settle disputes and make important decisions, although additional meetings could be called to resolve quarrels. Anyone could convene an assembly by sending an arrow to a neighboring farm. One man was selected to memorize the laws and was required to answer anyone who asked a legal question by reciting the appropriate law at the assembly.

VIKING WOMEN Women did the household jobs—mainly cooking, spinning, and weaving—with the help of thralls, or slaves. They also taught their children by telling them stories and riddles, orally passing on their traditions. Viking stories of their heroes, called sagas, were not written down until the 13th century.

There was somewhat more equality between the sexes in Viking communities than in the rest of Europe at the time. Viking women could own property, could divorce their husbands, and were in charge when the men were away. A wife's symbol of authority, which she carried fastened to her belt, was the key to the storage chest. The laws from the Viking Age make distinctions between free persons and slaves, but not between men and women. Many Norwegians see a connection between women's solid position during Viking times and their strong social position in Norway today. Norway has had an Equal Status Act—equivalent to an Equal Rights Amendment—since 1976.

Two Norwegian youths dressed as Vikings show how horns were blown to announce the return of a raiding expedition.

ONE NORWAY

Harald Fairhair (ruled 872–930) united most of western Norway after the Battle of Hafrsfjord in 872. (Some historians say it was in 892.) His son Erik Bloodaxe, so called because he murdered seven of his eight brothers, ruled from 930 to 935 and was succeeded by his surviving brother Haakon I Aldalsteinsfostre, also known as Haakon the Good. The new king successfully defeated Erik's sons, who, with aid from their uncle, the king of Denmark Harald Bluetooth, had attempted to overthrow Haakon. Haakon brought Christian missionaries to Norway from England, but his efforts to introduce Christianity to the people failed. He died in battle at Fitjar in 961. Erik's oldest son Harald II Eriksson took the throne and ruled oppressively. Conflict and power struggles erupted henceforth, and many regional leaders refused to give up their independence. Sweden and Denmark took advantage of this unrest and invaded Norway.

UNDER DANISH RULE In 995 Olav Tryggvason (ruled 995–1000), the great-grandson of Harald Fairhair, who had been brought up in England and baptized as a Catholic, ascended the throne. Olav I forced Catholicism on the Norwegians. This led Norwegian leaders to ally themselves with the Swedes and Danes to defeat and kill Olav I at the naval Battle of Svolder. The victors divided the land among themselves.

In 1015 another descendant of Harald Fairhair, Olav Haraldsson (ruled 1015–30), drove out the foreigners—Swedes and Danes—reunited Norway, and was acknowledged as King Olav II throughout Norway. He continued the Christianization of Norway, using the same ruthless methods

Olav Tryggvason became Olav I in A.D. 995.

28

as Olav I. As his power grew, he made many enemies among the nobles, who conspired with Canute II of Denmark to overthrow him. Olav II died in 1030 at the Battle of Stiklestad. Norway fell into Danish hands after his death.

Discontented with Canute's rule, the Norwegians began to think of Olav II as a hero despite his forced Christianization. A year after his death he was proclaimed a saint by the Roman Catholic Church. Saint Olav became the patron saint of Norway, and Christianity firmly rooted itself in the country. When Canute II died in 1035, Olav II's son Magnus was proclaimed Norway's king. Magnus I united Norway and Denmark under his rule in 1047. For the next three centuries, Norwegian kings ruled Norway.

AGE OF GREATNESS

Haakon IV's ascension to the throne (ruled 1217–63) ended a conflict between the church and the state that began in 1196 and escalated into civil war. He reunited the country and made peace with the church. He adopted a new rule of succession whereby the throne would be passed to the eldest son.

Haakon IV's reign is known as the Age of Greatness. He reorganized the government and maintained diplomatic contacts with many countries, including France and England. Under Haakon IV, the kingdom of Norway included all the western islands in the North Atlantic, and mainland Norway contained three regions that are now part of Sweden. Haakon IV also formally annexed Greenland in 1261 and Iceland in 1262.

Canute II of Denmark was also called Canute the Great because he made many wise laws.

Haakon was succeeded by his son Magnus Lagabøte. Magnus (Haakon V) revised the laws and persuaded the legislative assemblies to accept a common law for the whole country. When Norway's overseas possessions became hard to defend, Magnus sold the Hebrides and the Isle of Man to Scotland in 1266. This loss of territory signaled the start of the decline of Norway.

UNDER SWEDISH RULE

In 1319 Norway lost its independence when Haakon V died without male heirs. The throne went to the son of his daughter, who had married a Swedish prince. Thus Norway came under Swedish rule. Although Magnus VII ruled over both countries, he only lived in Sweden and neglected Norway.

After the bubonic plague, called the Black Death, killed half of Norway's population in 1350, the people demanded more consideration of their needs. To satisfy their demands, Magnus VII abdicated in favor of his son Haakon in 1355. Haakon VI was to be the last Norwegian king until 1905.

THE KALMAR UNION

Haakon VI's consort, Queen Margrete, who was also queen of Denmark, became queen of Norway when he died in 1380. In 1397, after Swedish nobles elected her to rule their country, Queen Margrete formally united Sweden, Denmark, and Norway under the Kalmar Union. Sweden broke away from the union in 1523, but Norway remained under the Danes for the next four centuries. In 1536 Denmark declared Norway a Danish province, and Norwegians lost the right to influence their country's affairs.

Akershus Fortress in Oslo was built during the reign of Haakon V. The king had several fortresses built because the kingdom's naval defenses were weak.

BACK TO SWEDEN

During the Napoleonic Wars of 1804 to 1814, Denmark allied itself with France. Britain set up a blockade to prevent ships with supplies from reaching Norway, and the people suffered. Denmark, defeated by Sweden in 1813, ceded Norway to Sweden in the Treaty of Kiel, but kept Norway's island colonies—Iceland, Greenland, and the Faeroe Islands.

Norway refused to recognize the treaty; instead, it declared its independence and adopted a Norwegian constitution on May 17, 1814. Sweden refused to accept this move and attacked and subdued Norwegian troops. In November 1814 the Norwegian parliament accepted King Charles XIII of Sweden as Norway's ruler, and he promised to uphold Norway's constitution. The two countries were to have one king and be allied in war, but in all other respects they were to be independent of each other in full equality. Under the union with Sweden, Norway was granted self-government.

King Haakon VII, Queen Maud, and Crown Prince Olav in 1910. Thirty years later, during World War II, King Haakon VII's stand inspired Norwegians and strengthened their will to resist the Germans. He became a symbol of resistance throughout the war, and during the long days of the German occupation the letter H and the number 7 appeared on mountainsides, snowbanks, and city walls.

INDEPENDENT NORWAY

The economy in the last few decades of the 19th century was good but could not keep pace with the population growth. There was growing unrest, and between 1866 and 1915 more than 600,000 Norwegians emigrated to North America in search of wealth and greater religious freedom. This prompted democratic reforms. The right to vote was extended to all men over 25 in 1898 and to women over the age of 25 in 1913.

The independence movement had been growing in Norway, and in 1892 negotiations began on the terms of the Swedish-Norwegian union. These proved fruitless, and in 1905 the entire Norwegian cabinet resigned. Norway's constitution only permitted the Swedish king to rule through the cabinet, so this left the king helpless. Norway no longer had a king of its own; therefore the union between Norway and Sweden no longer existed. Sweden initially refused to dissolve the union, but finally agreed to put the matter to a vote in Norway. Norwegians voted almost unanimously for independence, and Sweden recognized Norway as an independent country in September 1905.

The Norwegians voted to establish a constitutional monarchy, and elected Prince Carl of Denmark as their king. He became King Haakon VII of Norway, the first king of Norway since the death of Haakon VI in 1380. He ruled Norway until his death in 1957.

WORLD WAR II

Tensions escalated in Europe during the 1930s. As in World War I, Norway maintained a stance of neutrality. However, neutrality was of little significance when war broke out as both Germany and Britain recognized the strategic importance of Norway—from its coastal bases, German submarines would be able to operate in the North Sea. Realizing this, the Allies announced on April 8, 1940, that the British navy had mined the coast. Norway protested, but soon had worse things to worry about.

THE GERMANS ARE COMING Before dawn on April 9, 1940, the Germans invaded Norway and Denmark in a brilliantly executed surprise attack. Denmark capitulated in a few hours. Norway decided to fight, even though the Germans were superior in numbers and firepower. In the Oslofjord, Norway's old guns and torpedoes sank the large German cruiser *Blücher*, killing over 1,000 Germans on board. This delayed the Germans for a few crucial hours, and in that time King Haakon VII and the members of the cabinet and the parliament left Oslo by train for Hamar, 80 miles (129 km) north. The Bank of Norway's 50 tons of gold were also on their way north by the time the Germans overpowered Norway's resistance.

The parliament met in Elverum and unanimously decided that the government should have full powers to act on behalf of the nation, even if the king and cabinet were on foreign soil. The Germans demanded that Norway surrender and that King Haakon appoint the founder of the Norwegian Nazi party, Vidkun Quisling, as prime minister. The king declared he would rather abdicate. When the Germans started their bomb raids, the officials hid in the woods nearby. The king and the cabinet fled north, keeping just ahead of the Germans. The provisional capital was set up in the northern city of Tromsø then moved to London.

In December 1942 President Franklin D. Roosevelt of the United States called Norway "conquered and unconquerable." He added, "If there is anyone who still wonders why this war is being fought, let him look to Norway. If there is anyone who doubts the democratic will to win, again I say, let him look to Norway."

The Germans occupied Norway from 1940 until 1945.

GERMAN OCCUPATION Norway bravely fought the Germans for two months but eventually fell and was occupied until Germany's surrender in 1945. Membership in the Norwegian Nazi party increased from a few thousand in August 1940 to 43,000 in 1943 because of constant pressure to join.

Still, Norwegians expressed their resistance to the German occupation in many ways. As a gesture of loyalty to their country, some wore paper clips (a Norwegian invention) on their cuffs or lapels. Others wore flowers in their lapels on patriotic occasions. Many refused to ride buses where they might have to sit next to Germans or Norwegian Nazi party members. Some hid radios to tune in to BBC (Britain's official station) broadcasts, and others helped to write and distribute underground newspapers. By 1943 Norway had 60 underground newspapers.

Almost half of Norway's small Jewish population escaped the Nazis. Of the approximately 1,400 Norwegian Jews and 200 Jewish refugees from central Europe, 763 were deported to Auschwitz and other Nazi death or concentration camps. Only 24 of the deported Jews survived.

POSTWAR PERIOD

Germany lost the war, and Norway was liberated on May 8, 1945. King Haakon VII returned home to a big welcome. Twenty-four Norwegian collaborators, including Vidkun Quisling, were sentenced to death, and 19,000 others were imprisoned. During the cold war, Norway was anxious because it shared a border with the Soviet Union. Having learned that it could not rely on neutrality, Norway joined the North Atlantic Treaty Organization (NATO) in April 1949.

Norway had been left impoverished in 1945 because no trade was conducted during the war. An acute housing shortage existed because many buildings had been destroyed by retreating German troops and no building construction was started immediately after the war. The government gave priority to restoring Norway's productive capacity in consumer goods. By 1953 the north had been rebuilt and hydroelectric power had increased by 50 percent.

Vidkun Quisling gave the English language a new word—"quisling," meaning someone who undermines his or her country from within.

SABOTAGE!

Norwegians mounted many acts of resistance against the Germans. Those ranged from wearing King Haakon VII's emblem to running the Shetland Bus Service that ferried escapees to Scotland and carried weapons, radios, and special agents back to Norway.

One significant act of sabotage was the destruction of the heavy water (deuterium oxide) plant at Rjukan in Telemark. Heavy water is used in building atomic bombs, and Germany needed this plant in its race against the United States to build the first atomic bomb. On February 27, 1943, nine Norwegians climbed down a steep, icy mountainside, crossed a river, and ascended another dangerous mountain to the heavily guarded factory. Eluding German guards, they broke in, poured out the deuterium oxide, and planted explosives. Four of the nine remained safely hidden on Hardanger Plateau while the Germans mounted an extensive search for the culprits, and the others skied 250 miles (402 km) to safety in Sweden.

GOVERNMENT

NORWAY IS A CONSTITUTIONAL monarchy. The king is head of state, but his power is more symbolic than real. All three of Norway's kings since independence in 1905 have played a quiet role in government, privately questioning government leaders but generally refraining from public statements on policy.

THE MONARCHY

The king of Norway is a symbol of national unity. He is also the supreme commander of the Norwegian armed forces and the head of the Church of Norway.

Norway has been blessed with three kind, thoughtful, humble, and good kings since the country's independence from Sweden in 1905. At that time, Norway elected Prince Carl of Denmark as their king. He became King Haakon VII of Norway, the first king of Norway since the death of Haakon VI in 1380. By taking the name Haakon, he resurrected the line that had ended with the death of Haakon VI. King Haakon VII took as his motto "My all for Norway," and the two kings who came after him adopted the same motto.

King Olav V, who ruled from 1957 to 1991, succeeded King Haakon VII. Already a respected resistance hero, Olav soon became admired for his hard work and humble demeanor. Norwegians had even met him skiing outside Oslo without bodyguards. During the oil crisis in 1972, when the nation was asked to conserve fuel, King Olav set a personal example by taking the trolley when he went skiing and insisting on paying

Above: **A guard at his post at Royal Castle in Oslo.**

Opposite: **The main building of the Storting. This is where the parliament meets to make important national decisions.**

King Harald is an expert sailor.

his fare. He holds a special place in the hearts of Norwegians because he made his weakness public. He explained to the people of Norway that he suffered from dyslexia, which made giving speeches a challenge for him. Because he had made his handicap public, the people saw his handling of his difficulty as a symbol of human strength.

In 1991 King Olav, more affectionately known as the "people's king," died, and his son, King Harald V, the present king of Norway, succeeded to the throne. The health of the environment is a passion for King Harald. He was president of the World Wildlife Fund before becoming king and often stresses the serious need for worldwide conservation of the environment and Norway's special responsibility as a country with untouched wilderness areas.

THE ROLE OF THE ROYAL FAMILY

Royal succession in Norway had been in the direct male line, but the constitution was changed in 1990, permitting women born after that year to inherit the crown. After Crown Prince Haakon Magnus, who was born in 1973, his first child, Princess Ingrid Alexandra, who was born on January 21, 2004, will accede to the throne.

In addition to royal duties and political affairs, the royal family has always been active in sports, especially skiing and sailing—King Olav won a gold medal for sailing in the Olympics in 1928—and also is very involved in addressing social concerns. Princess Märtha Louise, the oldest daughter of King Harald V and elder sister to Crown Prince Haakon, was appointed a goodwill ambassador by the United Nations High Commissioner for Refugees in 1991. King Olav, despite the traditional royal reluctance to make public statements seeking to influence policy,

QUEENS OF NORWAY

From 1938 to 1991 Norway was without a queen. Before 1938 there was Queen Maud, wife of King Haakon VII, who had been frail most of her life. She was the daughter of King Edward VII and Queen Alexandra of Great Britain. Crown Princess Märtha, King Olav's Swedish-born wife and the daughter of Prince Carl of Sweden and Princess Ingeborg of Denmark, subsequently assumed the duties of the queen of Norway, but she died in 1954, before her husband succeeded to the throne. Having been without a queen since 1938, Norwegians were particularly happy when Sonja Haraldsen (*right*), a commoner, married Crown Prince Harald and, in 1991, became Norway's first Norwegian-born queen when her husband succeeded to the throne.

made a strong statement in 1987 in favor of maintaining an open society for the increasing stream of refugees into Norway. He reminded the country that he, too, had been an immigrant—arriving in Norway as a two-year-old when most of his family members were in England.

The royal family has had a strong tradition of being close to the people. Although some Norwegians see the monarchy as a contradiction to their ideal of equality, others point out that the king was elected in 1905. Until 1935, however, the Labor government of Norway was unfriendly to the royal family, often refusing to pass the palace budget or to attend dinner parties with the king.

World War II was a turning point in the population's acceptance of the royal family, as Norwegians were impressed with the courage of King Haakon VII in refusing German demands, and the future King Olav's bravery during the resistance. Today, however, while more than 60 percent of Norwegians approve of the monarchy, this is a significant drop from over 90 percent just a decade ago. A recent survey among teenagers 16 to 19 years of age reveals that the royal family holds little or no appeal to the younger generation.

ADMINISTRATIVE DIVISIONS

Norway is divided into 19 *fylker* (FEWL-ker), or counties. The city of Oslo is a *fylke* on its own. Each *fylke* except Oslo has a governor appointed by the king. The *fylker* are further divided into rural and urban *kommuner* (koo-MEW-ner), or districts.

Community councils, elected every four years, run the local districts. Each *fylke* also has a county council consisting of members of the community councils.

THE STORTING

Norway's 169-member parliament (increased from 165 to 169 after the

Norway's Storting (parliament) building was constructed over six years from 1860 to 1866.

2005 elections) is called the Storting (stoor-TING). Only the Storting has the power to enact and repeal laws, amend the constitution, impose taxes, appropriate money for government expenses, and keep a check on government agencies. It also appoints the Nobel Peace Prize committee.

Members of the Storting are elected every four years as representatives of their *fylker*, or counties, and political parties. Alternates are also elected, in case the elected member dies, is absent, or becomes a member of the cabinet.

All Norwegian citizens 18 years old and above can vote in parliamentary elections. Each of Norway's 19 counties elects four to 17 Storting members, depending on the size of the local population.

THE NOBEL PEACE PRIZE

Since 1901 the Nobel Peace Prize committee at the Nobel Institute in Oslo, which consists of five members appointed by the Storting, determines the winner of this prestigious award. The Nobel Peace Prize is given to "the person, or body, who has done the most or the best work for brotherhood among nations, for the abolition or reduction of standing armies, and for the holding and promotion of peace congresses."

Alfred Nobel, the Swedish inventor of dynamite, stipulated in his will of 1895 that the Nobel prizes in the sciences and for literature should be awarded by Swedish scholarly institutions, but that the decision on the peace prize should be left to a committee appointed by the Norwegian parliament. Although Norway and Sweden were still united at his death, Nobel's stipulation may have reflected his knowledge that the Norwegians were early supporters of the principle of international arbitration.

The Nobel Peace Prize committee is an independent body whose members are not usually also members of the Storting. The committee considers nominations from Norwegian peace organizations, previous winners, and various other groups. In recent years, nominations have climbed to almost 200 a year. The committee may refrain from awarding the prize altogether (it has done so 19 times), may give the prize to one person or institution, or award a joint prize. Several awards have been controversial, including the committee's decision in 1990 to award the prize to Mikhail Gorbachev, then president of the Soviet Union, which provoked another Norwegian group to award a People's Peace Prize to Lithuanian president Vytautas Landsbergis, who negotiated Lithuania's independence from the Soviet Union. Another controversy arose in 1994 when the Nobel Peace Prize was awarded to joint winners Shimon Perez, the former foreign and defense minister of Israel, late Israeli prime minister Yitzhak Rabin, who was assassinated in 1995, and late Palestinian leader Yasir Arafat, who died in 2004. Yasir Arafat's inclusion was the contentious issue, and because Arafat had engaged in terrorist activities, one member of the committee threatened to resign if Arafat was awarded the prize. The issue was finally resolved, and the three men were jointly awarded the prestigious Nobel Peace Prize for their work in trying to resolve the crisis between Israel and Palestine.

The Storting has only one house, but its members divide themselves into two sections—one-third sit on the Lagting (LAHG-ting), or law assembly, and two-thirds on the Odelsting (OH-duhls-ting), or heritage of the people assembly—to debate and vote on proposed legislation. A bill is first presented in the Odelsting. It is then considered for a second time in the Lagting. To become law, a bill must be passed by both bodies in succession and signed by the king when meeting with the cabinet. If the two bodies cannot agree on a bill, it can still be passed by two-thirds majority vote from the Storting and then sent to the king to be signed into law.

The ombudsman (OM-boods-mahn), or parliamentary commissioner, is consulted by people who feel they have been unjustly treated. There are ombudsmen in Norway for women, children, and military personnel.

THE CABINET

The cabinet consists of the prime minister and a number of other ministers (often about 18). Most cabinet ministers head a government department such as Foreign Affairs, the Environment, or Church and Cultural Affairs. Cabinet members cannot be members of the Storting, but may be called upon by the Storting to answer questions from the floor. Cabinet appointments must be approved by the Storting and usually reflect its political composition.

The cabinet meets several times a week. It is generally thought that the Norwegian prime minister, though having considerable influence, has less actual power than the U.S. president or the British or Canadian prime ministers.

When the United Nations established the World Commission on Environment and Development in 1983, it was headed by Norway's first woman prime minister, Gro Harlem Brundtland (right).

A WOMEN'S POLITICAL CHRONOLOGY

1884 – The Norwegian Association for the Rights of Women is founded. It works for improvements in women's education and in the legal status of married women.

1907 – Norwegian women get limited suffrage in parliamentary elections. All women who pay taxes, or whose husbands pay taxes, may vote.

1911 – Anna Rogstad becomes the first woman member of the Storting.

1913 – Norwegian women obtain the right to vote in national elections. Norway is the second country in Europe, after Finland, to extend full voting rights to women.

1956 – Eva Kolstad becomes president of the Norwegian Association for the Rights of Women, a position she will hold until 1968.

1960 – Signe Marie Stray Ryssdal becomes Norway's first woman counselor at law.

1970 – Ragnhild Selmer becomes Norway's first woman Supreme Court judge.

1971 – Inger Valle becomes Minister of Family and Consumer Affairs.

1972 – Eva Kolstad becomes Minister of Family and Consumer Affairs and Inger Valle becomes Minister of Government Administration.

1974 – Eva Kolstad becomes president of the Liberal Party, which was later disbanded.

1976 – Major Eva Berg becomes chief of the Joint Norwegian Military Nursing Services. Gro Harlem Brundtland becomes Minister of the Environment. Ruth Ryste becomes Minister of Social Affairs. Annemarie Lorentzen becomes Minister of Consumer Affairs and Government Administration. Inger Valle becomes Minister of Justice.

1979 – Norway's Equal Status Act prohibits sexual discrimination in all but religious communities.

1981 – Gro Harlem Brundtland becomes Norway's very first woman prime minister.

1986 – Gro Harlem Brundtland is reelected as prime minister.

1988 – The Equal Status Act is amended to require that the percentage of women on all publicly appointed committees and boards must be at least 40 percent.

1990 – Gro Harlem Brundtland is reelected as prime minister.

1990s – The three major political parties, Labor, Center, and Conservative, are headed by women.

2002 – Private companies are given until 2005 to voluntarily increase the share of women on their boards to at least 40 percent, otherwise sanctions will be imposed.

Norway has always been ahead of the times with regard to gender equality and women's rights, both in the social sphere and in politics. The first woman's suffrage organization in Norway was created in 1885, a year after the founding of the first woman's rights association.

POLITICAL PARTIES

Norway has several political parties. The Liberal Party is the oldest and was founded in 1884. The Labor Party has been the largest and most often in power since 1927, but over the past three decades it has faced increasing opposition from the Conservatives, who are often allied with the Center Party (formerly the Farmers' Party) and the Christian Democrats. Other parties in Norway include the Socialist Left and the Party of Progress.

Although the Labor Party has traditionally been the party in power, it lost its majority in 1981. Since then, Labor- and Conservative-led minority and coalition parties have alternated being the party in power. These shifts have made it increasingly difficult to form stable cabinets because the ruling party must build cabinets through coalitions, and rarely in recent times have parties completed their statutory four-year terms.

Trygve Lie, Norway's foreign minister during World War II, worked out of London since Norway was occupied by the Germans. He influenced the Norwegian government's decision to change its policy of neutrality to one of cooperation with Atlantic countries.

INTERNATIONAL COOPERATION

Norway has a tradition of active participation in international organizations that promote peaceful cooperation, including the League of Nations, its successor the United Nations, and the Nordic Council. Norwegians who have served in international organizations include Fridtjof Nansen (1861–1930), the League of Nations' High Commissioner for Prisoners of War; Trygve Lie (1896–1968), the first United Nations secretary-general, serving from 1946 to 1953; and Gro Harlem Brundtland, who was made chairperson of the World Commission on Environment and Development in 1983 and became director-general of the World Health Organization in 1998.

Since 1983 Norway has contributed around 1 percent of its gross domestic product (GDP) to foreign development aid, higher than the average contribution made by other industrialized Western countries and the United Nations' suggested 0.7 percent. Norway's contribution is regularly reviewed to ensure that it improves the situation of women and that it supports sustainable development—development that is ecologically benign and follows the guidelines of the World Commission on Environment and Development.

Norway is one of four countries that keeps a permanent force of soldiers ready for UN peacekeeping missions and has participated in all of them. Norway was a member of the UN Security Council from 2001 to 2002 and has also been active in the Nordic Council since the council's founding in 1952. The council coordinates cultural exchange, research, and social welfare benefits among Denmark, Finland, Iceland, Norway, and Sweden. One of the council's most significant results is the freedom of citizens of member countries to travel, work and reside within the member states countries without passports.

EU MEMBERSHIP

In 1994, despite active campaigning in favor of joining the European Union (EU) by the prime minister and other government officials, Norwegians voted for the second time not to join the EU. One reason may be Norway's bad experiences with political unions in its long history. A poll carried out in 2005, though, suggests that Norwegians are steadily warming to the idea of EU membership with almost 50 percent stating they would vote "yes" in a new referendum.

With almost all other European nations joining the European Union, Norway is in danger of being isolated in terms of trade agreements, political clout, and other benefits that might accrue from being part of a larger economic entity.

ECONOMY

SINCE WORLD WAR II, Norway's economy has undergone rapid industrial growth. The development of hydroelectric power and the discovery of oil in the 1960s have been instrumental in Norway's economic expansion. Although the economy slowed somewhat in the 1980s, Norwegians continue to enjoy one of the highest standards of living in the world.

The economy is dominated by private enterprise, but strict state regulations affect the private sector. The government regulates the disposal of industrial waste and supervises the activities of banks and insurance companies.

The Norwegian economy has undergone major changes in the past two decades. The traditional industrial and manufacturing sector has declined, while the service sector and modern industries, such as the petroleum industry, engineering, and data technology, have expanded. Today service industries constitute about 60 percent of Norway's gross domestic product (GDP), and employ about 74 percent of the workforce. Foreign trade, both import and export of goods and services, is an important component of Norway's economy. Norway's main trading partners include Britain, Sweden, Denmark, Germany, Japan, and the United States.

The Working Environment Act of 1977 requires employers to provide job security, limits working hours to nine hours a day, and forbids laborers to work more than 200 hours of overtime per year. In 2005 a new act was passed that maintains the principles of the 1977 act but with provisions to meet today's need for greater flexibility of working hours.

Opposite: **A worker sorts fish in a factory. Norway is a leading exporter of fish and fish products.**

Above: **The potential energy of numerous waterfalls provides the basis of Norway's hydroelectric power system.**

47

An offshore oil rig before it is towed out to sea. Small rigs, such as the one above, are used to drill wells at sea. When oil is discovered, a larger platform is established.

OIL AND ENERGY

When Norway sought to extend its territorial waters, geologists testified during hearings in Geneva in 1958 that there was very little possibility of finding oil, gas, or sulfur along Norway's continental shelf. It was not surprising, therefore, that when a representative from Phillips Petroleum in Oklahoma approached Trygve Lie in 1962 about the possibility of prospecting for oil off Norway, he replied, "I believe you must have made a mistake. Norway has no oil or gas." But in 1969 Phillips Petroleum struck oil in what is now known as the Ekofisk oil fields in the Norwegian section of the North Sea. By 1975 Norway was exporting oil products. In 1986 revenues from oil accounted for nearly 20 percent of the GDP, despite a drop in oil prices. Today, Norway is the world's third largest exporter of oil after Saudi Arabia and Russia.

Most of the current oil resources are located in the continental shelf off Norway's southwestern coast, but considerable reserves of oil are known to exist beyond the Arctic Circle. Although intensive exploration has been carried out in the Barents Sea, no discoveries have yet been made.

The Norwegian government controls much of the oil industry. After the discovery of oil, the Storting voted to limit annual production to conserve the oil fields. In 1972 Statoil, an oil and gas company, was created to oversee all aspects of the oil industry from exploration to processing and the sale of petroleum and natural gas.

Norway has two oil refineries, Mongstad near Bergen and Slagen near Oslo. Most of Norway's oil and gas are exported. Norway provides about 15 percent of Europe's gas requirements. For its own energy, Norway relies heavily on hydroelectric power. Norway produces more hydroelectric power in relation to its population than any other country in the world.

One of the many Norwegian natural gas tankers.

THE NAMING OF OIL FIELDS

Norwegians draw on their rich heritage of Old Norse myths and folktales to name many of their oil fields. Northwest of Stavanger is Odin; Frigg is on the median line between Britain and Norway. Near the Norway-Denmark divide is Valhalla, and Troll is found northwest of Bergen.

Less familiar names are Heimdall, northwest of Stavanger, named for the Old Norse god who guarded the rainbow bridge Bifrost and Sleipner, close to Frigg, which is named after Odin's fastest and eight-legged horse. Heidrun, named after the goat that stood on the roof of Valhalla and from whose udders came the liquor the fallen warriors drank, lies off the Nordland County. Gullfaks, west of the Sognefjord, is named both for a ship in Norwegian folklore that can sail as fast on land as at sea, and a horse that belonged to the giant Rungne in Old Norse myths.

A combine harvester works in a wheat field. Because only 3–4 percent of Norway's land can be cultivated, the country has to import most of its grain.

MANUFACTURING

Norway developed industries later than other European countries because it lacked coal to fuel factories. The development of hydroelectric power spurred rapid industrialization in the 20th century. Early industries depended on local raw materials, such as iron ore, timber, and fish. Since the discovery of oil in the late 1960s, a petrochemical industry has also developed.

Manufacturing contributes about 10 percent to the country's GDP. About half of Norway's factories are located near Oslo. Higher labor wages in Norway make Norway's products more expensive and less competitive on the international market.

Norway is one of the world's largest exporters of metal. Norway imports most of the raw materials it refines and exports these almost immediately after. Norway is one of the world's biggest producers and exporters of chemical products. Other manufactured products include machinery, pulp and paper, and textiles.

AGRICULTURE AND FORESTRY

Norway has only three main farming areas—the southeast, the southwest, and Trøndelag. These areas have a relatively favorable climate, flat fields, and fertile soil. Although Norway has developed from a mainly agricultural country into an industrial one, the government was running homesteading programs to encourage new settlement on the land as recently as the 1950s.

While the total agricultural area remains largely unchanged, the number of farms has decreased from 155,000 in 1969 to fewer than 60,000 today, employing less than 3 percent of the workforce. Most are dairy farms producing milk and cheese. The country produces enough livestock to meet its own needs and grows some produce such as potatoes, barley, oats, and wheat.

Norwegian farms are generally small: a typical farm has 22 acres (9 ha) of arable land and 124 acres (50 ha) of forest. Many farmers supplement their income by engaging in commercial forestry. Land owned by farmers contains about half the nation's productive forests, primarily in the counties of Nord-Trøndelag, Hedmark, Oppland, and Buskerud.

The government has traditionally subsidized farmers. The Storting decided in 1976 that all farmers should have the same annual income as an average industrial worker. However, these policies are being reviewed, and subsidies have been reduced. The government has promoted a policy of keeping people employed in all rural areas of the country in order to maintain Norway's ability to grow much of its food. As many of the government's agricultural policies are in conflict with the EU's farming regulations, most farmers oppose joining the EU.

Logs are floated down the Oslofjord. Wood, pulp, and paper exports make up about 11 percent of Norway's export earnings.

FISHING

Providing about 3 percent of the total global catch, Norway ranks as one of the world's top fishing countries, although the industry now earns less than 1 percent of Norway's GDP or national income.

Norwegian fishing crews catch about 2.7 million tons of fish per year, including cod, haddock, halibut, coalfish, and shrimp. Most of the catch is processed and exported. Fish farming of salmon and trout in the fjords and coastal inlets has become an important component of the industry, amounting to 500,000 tons in 2001. Most of Norway's hatcheries are located in the counties of Hordaland, Møre og Romsdal, and Trøndelag.

Because they are in danger of extinction, the government strictly regulates or forbids the fishing of herring and the hunting of seals. Following a five-year suspension of commercial whaling, Norway resumed minke (a small baleen whale) whaling in 1993.

Oceanor, Norway's ocean-monitoring body, aided the fishing industry by developing a highly sensitive electronic sensor to detect and measure the presence of 85 different types of algae in the ocean. Algae bloom can devastate fish farms. In 1988, for example, sensors registered a dramatic increase in the growth of a toxic alga in the North Sea. Oceanor advised fish farmers to tow their installations into areas of fjords not affected by the alga, and this saved salmon stock worth more than $130 million that year.

SHIPPING

With a coastline 34,000 miles (55,000 km) long, and a population concentrated along the coast, it is not surprising that Norway has a traditional involvement with ships and the sea. From catering just to its own transport needs, the shipping industry in Norway has grown into the country's third largest export industry. Norway is the fourth biggest shipping nation after Liberia, Panama, and Greece.

The shipping industry suffered a setback in the 1970s when oil prices rose. At the same time, developing countries, such as Panama and Liberia, became increasingly competitive and gained a growing share of the shipping market. The depression in Norway's shipping industry continued into the 1980s.

To meet the challenges, Norwegian shipping companies concentrated on new markets and operations that called for highly skilled maritime knowledge, and sharpened their marketing and consultancy skills. The Storting established the International Ship Register (NIS) in 1987 to assist shippers through a network of overseas stations.

A ship docks at a yard for repairs. In order to survive, many shipyards have become smaller and more specialized.

53

A seaplane waits at a jetty at Geirangerfjord. Seaplanes are often used to transport people from the fjords to the mountains for hunting or other sports.

TRANSPORTATION

Despite its rugged terrain, Norway has developed an efficient network of roads, railways, and water routes. Public transportation is well developed, including intercity buses and streetcars within cities. Three-quarters of Norway's 57,000 miles (92,000 km) of road are paved. Because of the uneven terrain, many roads curve along fjords and mountains and pass through tunnels and over bridges. The Norwegian road network includes more than 500 tunnels.

Historically, Norwegians depended on water transport, which was more efficient than land transport, given Norway's physical geography.

Coastal passenger and car ferries still provide a vital service for those living in western Norway, where roads are crisscrossed by fjords, and on the hundreds of islands.

Norway's rail system branches out from Oslo and connects all parts of the country. The railway extends to Sweden and Denmark. Norway has about 50 airports and relies increasingly on domestic airlines to reach the mountainous areas within the country.

A bridge in Tromsø. Although car density is high in Norway (2.2 inhabitants per car), highways and bridges are generally free of traffic jams.

ENVIRONMENT

NORWAY IS ONE of the least polluted nations. It is a country with few major environmental problems. However, the growth in industrialization and related activities in other nations have exposed its environment to potentially serious damage. In order to protect its own environment, Norway plays an active role in monitoring and managing environmental issues, not just locally but also internationally.

In May 2003 the Norwegian Minister of the Environment, Børge Brende, was elected chairman of the United Nations Commission on Sustainable Development, which takes the lead in ensuring the implementation of global sustainable development targets. Apart from proactive conservation efforts at the government level, ordinary Norwegians also enjoy a strong connection with nature. Given their lifelong love of the outdoors, most recognize the part they play.

POLLUTION

While air pollution in Norway's cities is not as serious as in other major world cities, it is still a concern. One of the most common causes of local pollution is nitrogen oxide (NO), produced mainly by road traffic, oil and gas extraction, and shipping. Per capita, NO emissions in Norway are among the highest in countries of the Organization for Economic Cooperation and Development (OECD). The other main cause is particulate matter generated by wood-burning stoves used during the winter months. Several government policies have been implemented to reduce the impact of road traffic on air quality. These include a tax on car ownership, refunds for scrapped cars, and public transport subsidies.

Air pollution is a pervasive problem that does not respect borders. Many hazardous chemicals are carried from afar by air currents and fall as acid rain. The most damaging elements of acid rain are sulfur and nitrogen.

When it comes to environmental issues, even the very young are given a voice. In each municipality, a "children's representative" is responsible for making the interests of children and youths heard.

Opposite: **Despite Norway's cold climate, it has many lush green forests.**

57

Norwegians use eco-friendly modes of transportation such as cycling to reduce pollution.

About 90 percent of the sulfur and nitrogen that is deposited in Norway comes from other European countries, created by the combustion of fossil fuels. A wide range of measures has been implemented to reduce and limit sulfur and nitrogen emissions. This has substantially reduced pollution, halving the acid rain deposit since 1980. However, despite this success, the damage caused to aquatic animals and plants is taking much longer to repair.

The highly sensitive ecosystems in southern Norway are at particular risk of pollution and erosion from acid rain, mainly because soils there are thin. While levels of heavy metal deposits such as lead have slowly decreased over the past two decades, the effects of mercury levels found in freshwater fish are evident. Contamination of lakes and rivers in the southernmost counties has caused many fish stocks to be depleted, and others such as salmon to be almost completely wiped out. The salmon stocks that survived are now endangered.

Norwegian forests have endured less damage in comparison with the lakes. In 1984 the Norwegian Monitoring Program for Forest Damage was established to keep a check on sulfur and nitrogen fallout. Following a decline in forest conditions due to air pollution and unstable climate in the 1990s, the forests appear to have recovered.

RECYCLING

Between 1974 and 2003, the average amount of household waste generated annually per person more than doubled to 980 pounds (365 kg). Despite this rise, the amount of waste incinerated and landfilled has decreased due to the practice of recycling embraced by most Norwegians. By 2003, 45 percent of household waste was being recycled, five times the amount just a decade earlier. The total volume of industrial waste has also been reduced over the years, mainly due to improved production processes that minimize waste.

Norwegians not only recycle their waste but also recycle their old cars.

The environmental impact of waste management depends on the volume and composition of the waste. Landfilling results in the release of greenhouse gases and hazardous chemicals that contribute to global warming. Incineration releases harmful chemicals and contaminated dust that pollute the atmosphere. Through legislation, taxes, and economic incentives, homes, businesses, and industries are continually encouraged to practice environmentally friendly waste recovery to reduce these harmful effects on the environment.

Innovation has played a part in Norway's successful recycling campaign. For example, in 1997 a recycling lottery was started. Consumers are asked to crush their empty drink cartons, write their names and addresses on them, and drop them into a recycling bin for entry into prize drawings. Since it began, the number of people recycling drink cartons has jumped from 30 percent to 70 percent.

To allow visitors to experience the Arctic beauty while minimizing any risk to the environment, all travelers to Svalbard must inform the local authorities of their trips in advance.

POLAR REGION

Once a virtually untouched wilderness, the Arctic is now under pressure from growing human invasion. As industry and tourists head deeper into the Arctic, monitoring and preserving this very fragile environment has become essential.

Svalbard's distinct landscape and ecosystem remain largely intact thanks to stringent measures aimed at protecting territories and natural species. The Svalbard Environmental Protection Act was implemented in 2001 with strict regulations to protect nature and historical sites. Under the act, all traces of human activity from 1945 or earlier are considered protected cultural remains. With 56 percent of Svalbard's land area protected, further conservation plans were passed in 2002 to extend legal protection by transforming other biologically productive areas into nature reserves.

Pollution in Norway's Arctic region comes mainly from distant sources. However, locally used organic environmental toxins such as polychlorinated biphenyls (PBC) and plant-protecting products have damaging effects on the reproductive system of mammals. Accumulated amounts of these toxins have been discovered in species at the end of the Arctic food chain such as the polar bear, seal, and herring around Svalbard, and these levels of toxins are among the highest in the Arctic.

Another major concern is global warming. Reports by the UN Panel on Climate Change warn that global warming will cause temperatures in the Arctic to rise more than the global average. The rise in temperature can cause substantial amounts of sea ice to melt and land such as Greenland in the Arctic Circle to flood due to the rise in the sea level. This can result in devastating consequences such as the contamination of freshwater supplies, coastal floodings, and unpredictable weather patterns.

MARINE LIFE

Just as pollution is a threat to Norway's rivers, lakes, and coastal areas, it has become evident over the past decade that it also has an impact at sea. Cold-water coral reefs found along the entire coastline of Norway and located about 6,562 feet (2,000 m) deep, are important for the ecosystem. They are crucial for fisheries, research, and marine resources, but they are the most vulnerable of marine environments. It is estimated that between 30 percent and 50 percent of coral reefs in Norwegian waters have been damaged or crushed by trawling activities.

In recent years authorities have taken measures to protect coral reefs. According to the World Wildlife Fund (WWF) in 2003, Norway is the only country to have implemented protection measures for cold-water reefs in European waters. That same year the WWF presented Norway its highest award for global conservation—the International Gift to the Earth Prize—in recognition of Norway's efforts in successfully stemming the deterioration of Norwegian coral reefs.

The Norwegians' efforts to protect the environment have allowed them to experience nature's wonders through encounters with wildlife such as the killer whale that could have been wiped out by unregulated and rampant pollution.

PROTECTED LAND

Forest and other woodland cover 39 percent of Norway's land area, amounting to about 30 million acres (12 million ha). Approximately 88 percent of this is privately owned, divided among more than 120,000 properties. Legislation, taxation, and economic support programs are in place to promote forest production and to sustain the forest as a thriving environment for plants, animals, and human recreation. To encourage optimal use of forest resources, and to reduce the use of fossil fuels, the government launched a five-year development program in 2000 aimed at promoting wood as an environmentally-friendly material suitable for a wider range of applications.

About 25 percent of total forest area is protected in order to safeguard natural resources, soil, and water against normal hazards and extreme climate conditions. Protected forests fall into several categories, including forest reserves and national parks.

There are 20 national parks in Norway, covering about 10 percent of the Norwegian mainland. In 1962 the Norwegian state started creating national parks with the purpose of preserving the rich diversity of the country's wildlife and natural environments, from the fjords to the mountains. The Norwegians are protective and proud of their parks as they view outdoor recreation as a large part of their cultural identity.

Visitors to the parks have opportunities to experience and admire wonderful varieties of plant, bird, and animal life. They can also hike through valleys and glaciers and enjoy panoramic views of the country's diverse and distinct landscapes. These include the gently rolling mountains of Hardangervidda, Norway's largest national park; northern Europe's highest peaks, at Jotunheimen National Park; and Europe's largest glacier, at Jostedalsbreen.

EVERY MAN'S RIGHT

Outdoor recreation is a big part of Norwegian culture. Everyone in Norway has public right of access to any uncultivated land in the countryside. This is according to an ancient unwritten law called *allemannsretten* (AWL-leh-mawns-reht-ten), or "every man's right." It is thought to date way back to the Viking age.

There is no law about this right, only restrictions that are outlined in the Outdoor Recreation Act. People are free to ramble through forests, hike up mountains, ski, cycle, or swim anywhere as long as no harm or disturbance is caused. This right also extends to cultivated land when it is frozen or snow-covered but does not apply if one is using a motor vehicle or engaging in sport fishing and hunting. With this freedom comes every individual's obligation to respect the natural environment.

In recent years increased commercial development has posed a threat to rights of access, particularly along coastal areas where homes and holiday cabins are being built. In response, the government is taking steps to safeguard the people's right to enjoy the natural landscape.

CULTURAL HERITAGE

Preserving Norway's heritage involves the protection of monuments, sites, and cultural environments. A total of 58,000 archaeological sites containing about 300,000 monuments have been registered in Norway. Each year about 1 percent of these are lost or damaged.

Norway's architectural heritage includes 375,000 buildings registered as being 100 years old or more, although only a small percentage are protected by the Cultural Heritage Act. Those that are protected include stave churches and other medieval wooden buildings.

Norway also extends protection of individual monuments and structures to include the surrounding environment. There are currently four such protected areas: the Havrå farm complex, the Ustein monastery, Kongsberg Silver Works, and the Sami settlement, Neiden. Other projects have been undertaken to safeguard important areas along the coast as well as restoration works.

Five Norwegian sites are on UNESCO's World Heritage List. These are the rock drawings of Alta, Urnes Stave Church, Bryggen (the old wharf) in Bergen, the mining town in Røros, and the Vega Archipelago.

NORWEGIANS

BY INTERNATIONAL STANDARDS, Norway has a small and homogeneous population. About 7 percent of the population is foreign born. The country has two indigenous ethnic minorities, the Norwegian Finns and the Sami.

NORWEGIANS

Most Norwegians are closely related to the Danes and the Swedes. The ancestors of these three Scandinavian peoples came from lands east of the Baltic Sea, from around the Mediterranean Sea, or from the European Alps. Over the centuries, Norwegians have intermarried with other groups.

Above and opposite:
Contrary to the popular image of all Norwegians being fair-haired and blue-eyed, many Norwegians have dark hair.

Norwegians pride themselves on their strong traditions of equality and humanitarianism. They are also fiercely independent and nationalistic, an attitude fueled by centuries of domination by others.

NORWEGIAN FINNS

The Kvener, or Finns, were involved in trade in northern Norway from the early 12th century. From the early 18th century through the 19th, some Finns came to Norway, looking for a more secure life in the fjords of Troms and Finnmark. Some were escaping marauding Russians. Others were fleeing the Swedish wars and the famine years of the 1860s. The best known Kven center, Vadsø on the far eastern coast of Norway, was called Vesi-Saari in Finnish, meaning "water island." In 1875 Finnish speakers made up 62 percent of the population, but today very little Finnish is heard in Norway, with only some 5,000 to 8,000 Finnish speakers.

"Our life is like a ski track on the white plateau which the wind erases before the day breaks."
—Paulus Utsi and Inger Huuva-Utsi, Sami poets and reindeer drivers (translated by Harold Gaski)

THE SAMI

The Sami (formerly called Lapps) have lived in Norway, Sweden, Finland, and the Kola Peninsula for thousands of years. Originally from Asia, they are of a darker complexion and are shorter than most Norwegians. Their language is related to Finnish. About 20,000 Sami—half of the total Sami population—live in Norway. In 1989 the Sami parliament opened, giving Sami a voice in issues concerning their status in Norway.

More than half of the Norwegian Sami live in the northern county of Finnmark—its name means "Sami borderland." In Old Norse, the Sami were called Finner, a reference to their abilities to locate game and find their way in wild country. Traditionally, the Sami are nomads who follow herds of reindeer. Many modern Sami have settled in fishing and farming communities, and many of these marry other Norwegians.

Like Native Americans, the Sami are eager for outsiders to see beyond the stereotypes based on museum displays and early travelers' accounts. The Romans recorded that the Sami dressed in animal skins and traveled on narrow pieces of wood–the earliest skis–and that Sami women hunted alongside the men. In the 15th century Norwegians began to invade Sami areas, depleting stocks of wild game. Some Sami responded by

REINDEER HERDING: A TRADITIONAL SAMI OCCUPATION

The life of the Sami reindeer-herding nomads has a regular pattern: a long stay at a winter base where herds feed on lichen under snow and on trees, a spring migration toward the coast with a pause for calving, a search for and travel to grazing areas on peninsulas and islands during summer, and in the fall, a reindeer roundup before heading back to camp. Nomadic Sami live in *lavvo* (LAH-voh), traditional skin tents, and travel on skis, the most efficient way of traversing snowy areas.

Reindeer-herding Sami face serious obstacles because their traditional migration routes are threatened and disrupted by dams, roads, national parks, sport fishing and hunting, mining, tourism, and military bases. Pollution is also a serious threat. The Chernobyl nuclear explosion in the Ukraine affected the Sami living in Trøndelag, as they were forced to slaughter their herds due to the high level of radioactivity caused by particulate fallout blown in by winds.

The Alta-Kautokeino River hydroelectric project proposed in 1970 became a major test of Sami rights. Sami, environmentalists, and advocates for ethnic and minority rights agitated against the dam, which would affect traditional Sami migratory routes. Despite the high level of mobilization against the project, the Storting and the Supreme Court approved it in 1982, and it was completed in 1987.

becoming full-time reindeer breeders and herders and organizing cooperatives based on kinship ties. Others settled on the coast and obtained food by hunting and fishing.

Only two-thirds of the Sami speak a Sami dialect, an unfortunate result of attempts by missionaries, agricultural experts, and schoolteachers from the 1850s to the 1950s to "Norwegianize" the Sami. In the 1960s the official government position shifted to a policy of accommodation and support. Research projects focusing on the Sami language and culture resulted in new curricula for all educational levels. Today, students may choose Sami as their first language in many communities. The Sami themselves have become involved in this Sami revivalism. There are now Sami newspapers, a Sami radio station, a major research library housed in Karasjok, and museums and theater groups.

THE ROLE OF WOMEN

Traditionally, Norwegian women fended for themselves and made their own decisions. In many rural communities the men used to go fishing off the coast for several months, leaving the women to run the farms and local affairs. This pattern continues today, with the men going off to work on oil rigs for two to three weeks at a time before returning home for a couple of weeks—except that today there are also women working on the rigs, and most women onshore are no longer on farms.

Even though Norway was the second country to give women the right to vote in national elections, and the first woman to sit in the Storting was Anna Rogstad in 1911, no woman became a cabinet minister until 1945, when Kirsten Hansteen was given the title of consultant minister but without a department to run.

Norwegian women entered the paid workforce later than other Scandinavian women. Even with the Equal Status Act, there yet remain differences in pay and the sharing of housework. However, with the gap between working hours of men and women closing, surveys show that women in Norway spend less time on housework today than 30 years ago. Many women have also traditionally chosen to be educated within the caring professions such as public health and social welfare, whereas more men have acquired economic and technical skills. This has given rise to strong patterns of occupational segregation, and today few women hold high-level jobs in industry or banking.

The University of Oslo has the world's first Department of Women's Law or Institute for Women's Law. A major research organization for women sponsors studies of issues that affect and concern women. It also started a Center for Women's and Studies and Gender Research in 1997.

EMIGRATION TO THE UNITED STATES

From 1840 until World War I, a growing flood of emigrants left Norway for the New World. Most emigrated because of rural poverty, leaving behind them small huts that have been called starvation cottages. Many were farm laborers who were paid only a few pennies a day, or children of farmers whose plots were too small or infertile to support an extended family.

Before the U.S. Immigration Act of 1924 restricted the flow of refugees, more than 800,000 Norwegians had migrated to the United States. In 1882 alone, 28,628 Norwegians emigrated. No other country, except Ireland, had larger numbers of its people moving to the United States.

Most of the immigrants settled in New York, California, and farming communities in the Midwest. Life in the early years was hard for these immigrants, but Norwegian-language newspapers, churches, and cultural associations helped keep the communities together. In Decorah, Iowa, at least two private colleges have Norwegian roots: Saint Olaf College and Luther College.

A number of private and public organizations have been founded to help Americans interested in researching their family history and lineage. Today, there are as many people of Norwegian descent living in the United States as there are Norwegians in Norway.

Although there had been some emigration of Norwegians to the early colonies in North America, the beginning of Norwegian emigration to the United States is dated from 1825, when the Restoration carried 52 Norwegians from Stavanger to New York.

Opposite: **A cruise officer from a ship touring Svalbard presents an image of vigor and competence.**

FRIDTJOF NANSEN

Fridtjof Nansen led the Norwegian delegation in Geneva from the first League of Nations' session in 1920 until his death in 1930. He played a heroic role in the bitter decade after World War I. He took on the assignment as League of Nations High Commissioner for Prisoners of War and successfully administered the repatriation of 450,000 former prisoners of war, most of whom had fought for Germany and its allies during World War I and were left forgotten in prison camps in Europe and Russia after the war.

Nansen also shouldered the even heavier burden of bringing relief to the millions of refugees and displaced persons uprooted in Europe and Asia during the war. When refugees could not cross international borders because they lacked proper identification documents, Nansen introduced a new form of supranational passport, the Nansen passport, which he persuaded more than 50 governments to recognize. He also moved them to accept quotas of refugees.

When Nansen was awarded the Nobel Peace Prize for his achievements in refugee relief in 1922, he was already in the midst of another assignment. At the request of the International Committee of the Red Cross, he personally led an immense famine-relief operation in the Soviet Union from 1921 to 1923. When the League of Nations did not support the project, he contributed the funds from his peace prize. Most diplomats said the task was impossible. Starting with tons of Norwegian cod-liver oil, Nansen defied all odds and saved the lives of an enormous number of people, reportedly ranging from 7 to 22 million people, more than half of them children.

Probably the greatest single achievement of Nansen's refugee work and humanitarian efforts was the resettlement and exchange of several hundred thousand Greeks and Turks following the defeat of the Greek army by the Turks in 1922. This rescue operation took eight years to accomplish and involved building new villages and industries for the resettled Greeks and Turks. His last project was particularly difficult—trying to assist in the resettlement of Armenians.

NORWEGIAN NEWCOMERS

Foreigners amount to about 7 percent of the total population of Norway. As of 2001, the majority of the immigrant population are from the Scandinavian countries such as Sweden and Denmark. Most other immigrants are from outside Europe, especially from Asia. In the 1960s Norway accepted migrant workers from Pakistan, India, Turkey, and Morocco. Since 1975, however, the government has placed a ban on immigration. Even so, Norway's immigrant population is contributing significantly to total population growth as the birth rate among ethnic Norwegians has declined.

Norway has a strong tradition of offering a home to asylum seekers and refugees. The country received a large increase in refugees in the

late 1980s as other European countries began restricting the entry of political asylum seekers. Many came from Chile, Iran, Sri Lanka, the former Yugoslavia, Poland, and Somalia. Norway was accepting between 1,000 and 4,000 refugees a year through the UN High Commission for Refugees, mostly from Iran and Vietnam. Although almost all were accepted in 1987, the acceptance rate has since dropped, due in part to Norway's tougher asylum policies over time.

Norway provides schooling in the foreigner's native language as long as four people are interested, but newcomers are expected to learn Norwegian. Those of school-going age are expected to attend school. Others are integrated through work programs and Norwegian language classes. Most immigrants live in Oslo or near Bergen and Stavanger.

While most Norwegians are comfortable with ethnic and cultural diversity, many expect non-Western immigrants to assimilate quickly into the Norwegian way of doing things. Some foreigners have experienced discrimination. Recognizing that Norway is changing, the government has begun to set up agencies to address immigrant issues and provide assistance to minorities, and is working to bridge cultural barriers.

Immigrants are given free lessons in the Norwegian language to help them adjust to the country and integrate into the Norwegian community.

71

LIFESTYLE

NORWAY ENJOYS ONE OF the highest living standards in the world. There is very little discrepancy in income because the taxation system takes from the wealthy and gives to the not-so-wealthy. This has resulted in a fairly equitable society where most people are in roughly the same economic class.

WORK

Norwegians are a hardworking people who also know where their priorities lie. Norway's parliament passed a Worker's Protection Act that limits maximum working hours to an annual

Above: **Like all other workers in Norway, rope makers in Bergen are protected by legislation.**

Opposite: **Norwegians relaxing and enjoying an afternoon in the city.**

average of nine hours a day. All night work is prohibited for day workers, as is working on Sundays and public holidays.

Child labor is strictly controlled, and children under the age of 15 are allowed only light work, such as that of messengers. Those under the age of 18 are not permitted to work overtime or at night.

Usual business hours are from 8 A.M. to 4 P.M., with only a short break of about 20 minutes for lunch, usually of sandwiches brought from home. These working hours are faithfully followed in winter, but in summer, office workers often leave work an hour earlier in order to enjoy the sun as much as possible. Norway has also legislated a four-week vacation with full pay for all workers. This means workers would enjoy more time for family activities and leisure pursuits. Striking a balance between family time and work is a deliberate policy in Norway. Both parents can share 42 weeks of fully paid leave when they have a baby. The father has to take at least four weeks of these or forfeit them.

Every family member is protected by a comprehensive package of health and welfare benefits.

A WELFARE NATION

Norway is a world leader in state-funded health care, housing, employment benefits, retirement plans, and other services. Norwegian laws guarantee the right to employment, a place to live, education, social security, and health and hospital benefits. The welfare system is funded through taxes and insurance. Recently, however, there has been discontent with the high level of taxation, and Norwegians have begun to question whether they want to continue subsidizing lower-income families, usually immigrants.

Families with children under 18 receive a yearly allowance per child, while single parents receive benefits for one child more than is actually supported. Aid is also available to help these families pay for housing. This has ensured a minimum standard of living for all Norwegian citizens.

Norwegians are required to buy into the social security national insurance program, which includes retirement funds, job retraining, and unemployment benefits. Free medical care and disability benefits are part of the plan. The cost of the program is borne jointly by workers, employers, and national and local governments.

A SPECIAL PLACE FOR CHILDREN WITH DISABILITIES

Norway has made special provisions for disabled children. The official educational policy is to integrate children of all capabilities into the regular educational system rather than stigmatizing those who are differently abled by segregating them. Such children are encouraged to attend normal classes, usually with a therapist present. This is in line with Norway's policy to ensure equal educational opportunities for all.

This integration has helped able-bodied Norwegian children to learn to be patient and to appreciate their classmates of different abilities. However, this integration may come at the expense of exceptionally gifted children. Norway's equal educational opportunities policy effectively means that disadvantaged and slower learners are given a helping hand but gifted children are not given the opportunity to excel and develop at an accelerated pace.

Norway has realized that a balance between the needs of the disabled and those of the gifted is necessary, and it is striving toward reaching an equilibrium.

HEALTH

Norwegians have no severe health problems apart from those common to wealthy countries, namely heart disease and cancer. Children receive a program of vaccinations, and everyone undergoes periodic tests for tuberculosis.

In 2005 the average life expectancy for Norwegians was 79 years, a gain and extension of more than 25 years over their ancestors in the 1890s, who could only expect to live for 52 years. Norway also has one of the lowest infant mortality rates in the world, at 3.7 deaths out of every 1,000 babies born. Norway is now experiencing a shortage of retirement and nursing homes because more Norwegians are living longer. Officials project that the number of persons aged 67 years and older will double between 2002 and 2050. As with most industrialized countries, Norway has a very low birth rate. More women who choose to conceive are content with just having one or two children.

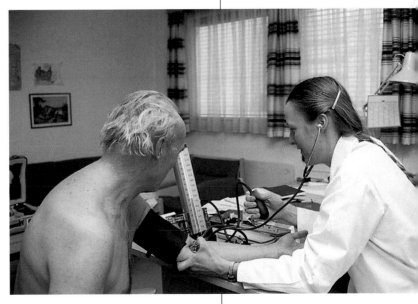

A doctor takes a reading of her patient's blood pressure. Health services in Norway are partly financed through compulsory membership of all Norwegians in the national insurance program.

If this little girl does not like the name her parents gave her, she can change it. Norwegian law has made it easy for people to change their names—once.

BIRTH AND BAPTISM

Although women do visit clinics for prenatal care before their babies are born, they turn to midwives to help them through the nine months of pregnancy. When it is time for the baby to be born, the local midwife accompanies the woman to the hospital and places her into the care of the hospital midwife, who supervises the birth. New mothers are not pampered in Norway—childbirth is seen as a difficult procedure, not a debilitating ordeal.

One of the first ceremonies a child undergoes is baptism. Baptism marks the child's entry into the Lutheran Church of Norway, the state religion since 1539. Family and close friends are usually invited, and two married couples are selected as the child's godparents. Theirs is a lifelong task as they are expected to be the child's moral guides, to ensure that he or she grows up with sound values and tolerant attitudes.

Baptism is also the ceremony at which a child is named. Naming a child in Norway used to follow a strict pattern. The eldest son was named after his paternal grandfather, and the next son after his maternal grandfather. The eldest and second daughters were named after their paternal and maternal grandmothers, respectively. Then the names of great-grandparents were used, or relatives who had passed away. Today, however, Norwegians are free to choose their children's names. They may make the selection from a book of names, or name their children after friends or relatives. Often a child is given a grandparent's name as his or her middle name.

CONFIRMATION

This is one of the most important ceremonies for Norwegians who belong to the Church of Norway. Confirmation represents the 14- or 15-year-old's acceptance of a Christian heritage and the principles of the Lutheran Church of Norway.

All those wishing to be confirmed attend a two-month preparatory course, during which they are given a thorough grounding in the principles of the church. If they decide they can abide by these principles, they then go through the confirmation ceremony, in which they publicly declare that they wish to remain a part of the Lutheran Church. The confirmation ceremony takes place in church and is attended by friends and family. There is usually a large celebration after the ceremony, and friends and relatives come from all over to participate in the occasion and celebrate with the family.

THE *KVINNEGRUPPE*

The *kvinnegruppe* (KVIN-nuh-GREW-puh) is a gathering of women interested in discussing women's issues and current literature. Members are mostly professional women in their mid-20s to mid-30s, although many are homemakers and university students. These women are not radical feminists, but are simply women interested in airing their opinions about the policies and issues that affect them. The group is not action-oriented, but it does serve as an outlet for women to discuss matters that concern them and to listen to alternative points of view or gain support for their views. It is also a wonderful opportunity for interaction with like-minded women, and most members enjoy relaxing with a cup of coffee in a pleasant atmosphere. There is a *kvinnegruppe* in almost every district.

Women's groups are not restricted to the kvinnegruppe. The husmorlag (HEWS-moor-lahg) is a neighborhood group of women who do projects of common interest: running preschool centers; helping the elderly; doing charity work; or learning a language. Notices of their activities are posted in community centers, churches, and neighborhood stores.

EDUCATION

A *barnehage* (BAR-neh-HAH-guh) is a kindergarten for children ages 4–7. It teaches counting, singing, crafts, socializing skills, and discipline. The *førskole* (FEWR-skool-uh), a special preschool for children aged 6, prepares them for entry into an elementary school at age 7.

As education is free up to university level, nearly everyone in Norway can read and write. Children in Norway begin school at age 7, and basic education lasts nine years. Children go through six years of elementary education, followed by another three years in junior high school. In order to ensure that all Norwegian children have equal educational opportunities, the Norwegian school system decides on one elementary curriculum and one method of teaching for the entire country. The curriculum focuses on nature study, physical education, social studies, and Christianity, in addition to math, science, Norwegian, and foreign languages.

After junior high many students proceed to three years of high school education. This could be obtained at a gymnasium, which focuses on general education in preparation for a course of study at a university, or a vocational school for occupational training.

Norway has six universities, located in Oslo, Trondheim, Bergen, Tromsø, Ås, and Stavanger. The country has several colleges, all funded by the state.

THE COMMISSIONER FOR CHILDREN

Parliamentary debate in the 1970s on how the country could best address children's needs in a democracy where children have no vote resulted in the creation of the children's ombudsman, the Commissioner for Children.

The ombudsman's duties are to promote the interests of children and to monitor the conditions under which children grow up. The ombudsman comes under the Ministry for Children and Family Affairs. The work is twofold: gathering information from all levels of society and then approaching the authorities with problems, criticisms, and proposals for change.

The ombudsman has a high public profile as the children's spokesperson on issues important to them. On a radio and television show, the ombudsman reads out the latest cases handled and letters received from children about issues as diverse as dangerous play areas and living in families with alcoholics.

Klar Melding (*klahr MEHL-ding*), *or clear message, is a toll-free hotline to the ombudsman's office for all Norwegians under 18 to ask any question or present any problem. These questions are then answered on a radio and television show.*

HOUSES AND GARDENS

These well-preserved houses built for German merchants of the Hanseatic League, a medieval trading association, are now historical sites. Modern homes are usually located in the suburbs.

Many Norwegians living in cities join housing cooperatives called *borettslag* (BOOR-ehts-lahg), which finance housing projects. Single residences or apartments are then rented to its members, who pay a deposit to join in addition to the monthly rent. It is a first-come-first-served system, and some Norwegian parents sponsor their children's membership in a *borettslag* years before it is needed in order to give them an early

start in the waiting line. If a member wishes to leave such a cooperative and to sell his or her share in it, the board of the cooperative must approve the sale—in this, as well as in other respects, the housing cooperative is like an exclusive club.

Attached row houses and apartments in condominiums are popular in urban areas, and single houses are common in the country. Singles prefer one-room apartments, or *hybel* (HEE-behl), in private houses or apartment buildings. Summer homes near the sea or in the mountains are popular with urban Norwegians. These are usually simple shacks with a garden where the family enjoys outdoor meals in fine weather.

Norwegians have a reputation for being self-sufficient, particularly when work is to be done in their own house or garden. Tasks such as painting, wallpapering, or fixing the roof are tackled with relish.

Gardening is seen as a way to commune with the soil. Most cities have a local gardening association and plant nurseries that give seasonal planting advice. In Oslo a public area is set aside for those who wish to indulge in summer gardening.

RELIGION

OVER 90 PERCENT OF NORWEGIANS are Christian, and of these the majority are members of the Church of Norway, which is Evangelical Lutheran. Norway's constitution guarantees religious freedom for all.

THE CHURCH OF NORWAY

The origins of the Lutheran Church go back to Martin Luther (1483–1546), a German Catholic priest who objected to some Catholic practices and started the revolution known as the Protestant Reformation. Through his actions and writings, Luther ushered in not only Protestantism, but also conditions for a revolution in economic, political, and social thought.

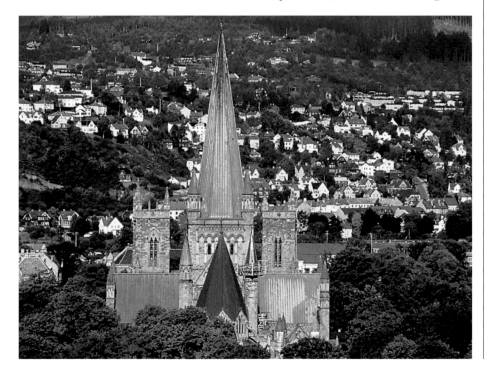

Left: **Nidaros Cathedral in Trondheim, a city founded a thousand years ago, is a historical landmark in Norway.**

Opposite: **Built in 1180, the Borgund church is the largest, oldest, and most ornate stave church in Norway.**

The architecture of a church in a rural area is usually very simple.

By the mid-16th century most of northern Europe was Lutheran. Lutheranism reached Denmark as early as the 1520s, but it was not until 1539 that the Danish Church was established with the king as the head and the clergy as leaders in matters of faith. As it was part of the Kalmar Union with Denmark and Sweden at the time, Norway followed suit.

Lutherans, like other Protestant denominations, believe in the divinity and humanity of Jesus Christ and in the Trinity of God. They have two sacraments—baptism and the Lord's Supper (or communion). The congregation is led by either a pastor or a lay person, who is elected from the membership of a council made up of a congregation's clergy and elected lay persons.

The Church of Norway is state funded, and the government appoints pastors and church officials. In 1956 the Storting passed a law allowing women to become pastors; the state named the first female pastor in 1961.

The majority of Norwegian Lutherans are baptized, confirmed, married, and buried in religious ceremonies, but fewer than 20 percent of Norwegian adults attend church more than five times a year.

OLD NORSE GODS

The mythology of northern Europe goes back to a time long before the Vikings. Viking poets and storytellers retold many tales, often with conflicting details, about the gods and goddesses who lived in a heavenly place called Asgard.

Chief among the pagan gods were Odin (or Woden), god of war and wisdom; Thor, the god of thunder and storms and the slayer of trolls and giants; Frey, the god of fertility and peace; Tyr, the bravest fighter among them all; and Freya, the earth goddess and patron of pleasure.

Odin was the god of poetry and magic as well as war, and the early kings of Norway were fond of tracing their ancestry back to him. Odin sent young women called Valkyries to lead warriors who died in battle to the Viking heaven, Valhalla. This was a huge hall with 640 doors, each so wide that 960 *einherjer* (EIN-hair-yair), meaning the chosen ones who were admitted to Valhalla, could pass through them side by side.

Odin, who had sacrificed one of his eyes in exchange for a drink from the Well of Knowledge, had two ravens, Hugin and Mugin, as companions. The birds set out each dawn to fly all over the world and returned every night to report on all that had happened during the day. Odin's wife, Frigg, the mother goddess, spun, on her spinning wheel, gold thread that was woven into summer clouds on her loom.

Although Odin was the chief god, Thor was more popular because of his power over the weather. His symbol was the hammer, with which he made the great noise of thunder. Frey, the god of fertility and harvest, had to be appeased by the Vikings. To please Frey they scattered bread and poured wine on the ground when they sowed their seeds.

A bronze image of Thor and his hammer. Many Vikings wore hammer pendants around their necks and took the name Thor as part of their own, such as Thorfnn or Thorvald. English names for some of the days of the week derive from Old Norse gods: Odin (or Woden) yields Wednesday, Thor Thursday, and Frey Friday.

NORWAY'S CONVERSION TO CHRISTIANITY

During their expeditions overseas, the Vikings came in contact with Christian Europe. Some Vikings pretended to convert in order to get trade benefits, but those who settled abroad usually became Christians. Norway, however, remained faithful to the old gods for a long time. Christianizing the country took 200 years and was marked by much bloodshed.

THE MISSIONARY KING Before his death, Harald Fairhair bequeathed the realm to his son Erik Bloodaxe (ruled 930–935). When Erik was forced from the throne, Harald's younger son, Haakon (ruled 945–960), who was only 15, returned to Norway and united most of the country.

Haakon, who had been educated as a Christian at the court of King Athelstan in England, was Norway's first Christian king, and he wanted Norway to become a Christian country. He was so well liked that he was called "Haakon the Good." However, he made little headway in establishing Christianity. Instead, the people insisted that he participate in their old rituals.

OLAV TRYGGVASON The grandson of Harald Fairhair, Olav Tryggvason, claimed the throne of Norway in 995. As a child, he fled to Russia with his mother to escape from being killed by Erik Bloodaxe. From there, he began a career as a Viking at an early age, conducting raids from the Baltics to the British Isles. Olav was so famous that he was able to collect large fleets of ships for his part in Viking attacks against England in the 980s and 990s. In England he accepted Christianity and was confirmed by the Bishop of Winchester under the sponsorship of King Æthelred the Unræd (or Ethelred the Unready)—whom he had recently attacked. When he arrived in Norway in 995, Olav was immediately accepted as king in Trøndelag, though more gradually by the rest of the country.

Viking sagas give an account of a feast, known as the "blood offering," where the people wanted Haakon to follow a traditional ritual and to eat horseflesh and drink the blood in which the flesh was cooked. Haakon refused but compromised by opening his mouth over the steam. This did not satisfy the people, however, and at the next sacrifice he was required to eat some horse liver.

Norway's conversion to Christianity

Aided by English missionaries, Olav was determined to bring Christianity to the people of Norway. Around the year 1000 he sent a Catholic priest with Viking Leif Eriksson to Greenland to convert the settlers. Many of the settlers converted, but for Olav, in Norway, conversion was a struggle. Many Norwegians still believed in the old gods, and so Olav resorted to force. Using the methods of a Viking raider, Olav sailed along the coast demanding that the *tings* (tings), or assemblies, submit and accept baptism. Those who refused were tortured or put to death. He forbade the worship of the old gods, destroyed their temples, and built the first church in Norway, in a village in Moster, south of Bergen. Olav's methods gained him many enemies and he was killed at the Battle of Svold in 1000.

NORWAY'S ETERNAL KING Olav Haraldsson landed in Norway with two shiploads of fighting men in 1015. Within a year he had defeated Olav Tryggvasson's enemies and had himself proclaimed king of Norway. He extended his rule into parts of east Norway, which until then had been under local chieftains, and fought the Danes in the Vik area in the Oslofjord. By 1020, Olav ruled all of Norway as King Olav II.

Olav II also set out to convert Norway, by force when necessary. In this last struggle between the old faith and the new, Christianity finally won. If the farmers refused to accept Christianity at a *ting*, Olav forced them to change their minds through violence, murder, and fire.

Like Olav I, Olav II's methods won him enemies. The former chieftains, backed by the king of Denmark, attacked Olav II in 1028. Olav fled to Russia but returned in an attempt to win back his kingdom. Finally the opposing forces met in 1030 at a farm called Stiklestad near Trondheim. Outnumbered two to one, Olav was killed and his followers defeated. His body was secretly carried to the city of Trondheim and buried in the sandbank of the River Nid. He was later canonized as Saint Olav.

According to legend, Olav Haraldsson was waiting in Spain for favorable winds to take him through the Straits of Gibraltar when he dreamed that a man approached him and said, "Return to your home, for you are to be king of Norway for time immemorial." On his way home, Olav spent the winter in Normandy, France, and was converted to Christianity there.

PATRON SAINT OF NORWAY

After the death of Olav II, people began to recall that there had been wondrous signs during the Battle of Stiklestad, and reports of miracles occurring at Olav's grave began to spread.

One year after the battle, Olav was declared a saint. Now Norway had its own patron saint, solidifying its ties with the rest of Europe. Olav was acknowledged as a saint throughout Europe and as far away as Constantinople. Churches were built in his honor by the hundreds, not only in Norway but also in Rome and London, where there were at least six built in his name. The day of his death, July 29, became a great religious festival in the north of Europe. Even today, the date is celebrated in Trondheim with reenactments of the battle and other medieval scenes.

Olav Haraldsson began his Viking career when he was 12 years old. He fought in the Baltics, in western Europe, and in England, where in 1009 he attacked London and helped to tear down London Bridge with grappling irons. This event is remembered in the nursery rhyme, "London Bridge Is Falling Down."

Saint Olav had become both a Christian martyr and a champion of national liberty. Down through the ages, his memory lives on as the symbol of a united, independent Norway. He has become the "Eternal King of Norway."

Within five years of his death, two of Olav's former enemies traveled to Russia and brought back his 11-year-old son Magnus to be king. The foreign rulers fled the country.

After the death of Saint Olav, Christianity came to be accepted as the religion of the country. The old communal beer feasts were incorporated into the observance of holy days. The beer was now blessed and the first cup drunk "in honor of Christ and the Blessed Virgin for good years and peace." However, traces of the old beliefs were slow to disappear. Some forms of nature and ancestor worship lingered on for centuries, and there was no serious attempt to convert the Sami until the 16th century.

OTHER CHRISTIAN CHURCHES

Besides the Lutheran Church, several other denominations have adherents in Norway. These include the Pentecostals, Lutheran Free Church members, Methodists, Baptists, Roman Catholics, and Jehovah's Witnesses. Many of these denominations migrated from other European countries.

The Pentecostal movement gained prominence in the early 20th century in the United States and spread rapidly to all parts of the world. Pentecostal services are enthusiastic and rousing, with an emphasis on music and congregational participation. The Pentecostal movement is attractive to people interested in social reform.

OTHER RELIGIONS

Political instability and economic hardship in nearby lands resulted in a large influx of immigrants into Norway. These immigrants and minority groups brought with them other religions, including Islam, Judaism, Buddhism, and Hinduism.

A Sami congregation in a church in Kautokeino. The majority of Sami are members of the Church of Norway.

LANGUAGE

NORWEGIAN IS PART OF the Germanic family of languages and draws from many European sources. Mountains and fjords historically isolated Norwegian settlements from one another, resulting in numerous dialects existing in Norway. The different dialects are very similar, and all Norwegians can understand each other, regardless of what dialect they speak.

The Sami have their own language, which is part of the Finno-Ugric language family. There are three major Sami dialects in the world, two of which, North Sami and South Sami, are spoken in Norway.

There are estimated to be as many as 8,000 Norwegian Finns in Norway, who are Finnish speakers. Finnish is part of the Finno-Ugric family of languages and is therefore distantly related to the Sami language. Finnish speakers in Norway are mostly bilingual in Finnish and Norwegian.

Above: **The scent shop sign for** *henne* **(HEN-nuh) and** *ham* **(hamn—commonly spelled** *han* **today) indicates that it sells both female and male scents.**

Opposite: **Norwegian and English are related, but visitors to the popular resort of Geilo are given directions mostly in English.**

NORWEGIAN

Norwegian and English are related languages because both evolved from a common North Germanic language. English, German, Dutch, and Frisian (a language with variants of it spoken in the Netherlands and Germany) split off long ago, leaving Common Scandinavian, which was spoken from about A.D. 550 to 1050. Common Scandinavian was the parent language of six official, literary languages in Scandinavia—including Danish; Bokmål (BOOK-mawl), which is book Norwegian or Dano-Norwegian; Nynorsk (NEE-noshk), or new Norwegian; Swedish; Faeroese, a West Scandinavian language; and Icelandic—plus a great variety of spoken dialects. Norwegian became a written language in the early 12th century when the Latin alphabet was introduced in Norway.

Most newspapers are published in Bokmål.

Two forms of the Norwegian language, Bokmål and Nynorsk, are officially used. Bokmål developed during Norway's 400-year union with Denmark and is mainly spoken in large towns, which were strongly influenced by Danish rule. Spoken Bokmål sounds very different from Danish, but the written form is nearly identical. Created in reaction to Danish rule, Nynorsk dates from the mid-1800s. It combines elements from major rural dialects to produce a more distinctly Norwegian language.

In the 20th century Norwegian language experts sought to streamline the two official languages into one, called Samnorsk (SAHM-noshk), or common Norwegian. The combined form was intended to simplify communication between urban and rural areas and in the mass media, which now alternate between the two forms. Some Norwegians, however, feel strongly that Bokmål and Nynorsk—as well as the many dialects that influenced them—are part of Norwegian heritage and should not be allowed to vanish. Since 1925 all government officials have been required to answer letters in the language in which they are written. As such, bureaucrats must be competent in both forms of the language. Local school boards decide which form will be used in their elementary school, and the current split is about 20 percent Nynorsk and 80 percent Bokmål.

The language question has been a political and economic issue for at least 150 years in Norway.

BOKMÅL VS. NYNORSK

With the many influences on Norwegian throughout the centuries, two approaches to creating a modern Norwegian language have developed. One model, Nynorsk, sought to build a language as close as possible to what Norwegian might be had it not been under Danish domination for centuries. Ivar Aasen (1813–69), a linguist and poet, analyzed western Norwegian dialects and formulated a written form for Nynorsk in *Norsk Grammatik* (*Norwegian Grammar*, 1864), and in *Norsk Ordbog* (*Norwegian Dictionary*, 1873). Since Aasen drew on rural dialects, Nynorsk has great strength in poetic and literary terms describing nature and personal matters. Nynorsk is not the native language of any Norwegian speaker, and it never became the first language of Norway, but it has long had a group of supporters who associate it with a more democratic national consciousness and who see Bokmål as a form of Danish.

Bokmål, earlier called Riksmål (RIKS-mawl), language of the kingdom, used Danish as the base and Norwegianized it through changes in spelling, vocabulary, and pronunciation. Bokmål built on the speech and writings of the educated urban population. In 1856 Knud Knudsen (1812–95), a linguist and educator, advocated a step-by-step Norwegianization of Danish spelling, a policy followed by such leading writers of the time as Henrik Ibsen. Over the years, Bokmål has retained much of the Danish vocabulary, while accepting some of the Norwegian pronunciation. Bokmål is the language taught abroad as Norwegian today.

After spelling reforms in 1907, 1917, 1938, and 1959, intended to bring the two languages closer, some hoped for the merger of the two languages into Samnorsk. Students reacted in 1960 by burning books translated into Samnorsk. Samnorsk was never accepted, and today Bokmål and Nynorsk exist side by side.

RUNES

Runes are angular letters that make up the ancient runic alphabet, one of the earliest forms of Germanic writing. Every rune had a special name, and these names are known through the oral traditions recorded in Anglo-Saxon manuscripts. The 24 runes of the early runic alphabet were divided into three groups of eight runes each. Each group was called an *ætt* (eht) in Scandinavia, which is thought to mean a group of eight. Later, the runes were called *futhark* (FEW-thahrk), which is the word spelled by the first six letters.

RUNIC WRITING

The oldest written examples of any Germanic languages are the runic inscriptions in Scandinavia. About 3,500 runic inscriptions have been found on objects as diverse as weapons, spear blades, and brooches. The most enduring examples have been the rune stones.

Rune stones are solid stone slabs carved with runic inscriptions and ornamental designs. The earliest known stone dates back to A.D. 300. Very little is known about the origin of rune stones, but experts believe they were linked to magic and sorcery, and perhaps religious rituals. It is thought that the common material for runic inscriptions was wood, but none has survived. Surviving rune stones show two runic alphabets: the older, used from the third to the ninth centuries, had 24 letters, and the latter had only 16 letters, a simplification of the earlier alphabet.

Runic inscriptions were often set within a decorated snake or dragon coil. Occasionally other ornamental designs were used as well. Stone engravers sometimes took it upon themselves to include additional information to the commissioned text. Much of our information about the political, economic, and cultural conditions of those times comes from these rune stones. The stones also tell of Viking journeys as far away as Byzantium and Baghdad, as many were memorials to someone who died on the journeys. It is from the pictures on these stones that we know Old Norse legends of Sigurd, the dragon slayer, and Thor, the thunder god.

THE SAMI LANGUAGE

The Sami language is not Germanic, as Norwegian is, but is part of the Finno-Ugric language family, which is related to Finnish and Hungarian. Sami speakers are divided into three main dialect groups: North Sami, mostly spoken in northern Norway, Finland, and Sweden; East Sami, which includes Inari and Skolt in Eastern Finland and Kola Sami from the Kola Peninsula; and the least common, South Sami, still represented by a few scattered speakers from central Norway to north-central Sweden. Each of these dialect groups has various subgroups. Sami dialects are so different from one another that a member of one dialect group cannot understand a member of another. When Norwegian Sami of different dialect groups meet, they communicate in Norwegian.

North Sami has a literary tradition that began with the 17th century Swedish Sami Bible and other religious translations. In the mid-20th century, elementary schools that used Sami as the language of instruction were found in many larger North Sami communities. The Sami in Norway use a special system of writing that was created to accommodate a wide range of variations in dialects.

The vocabulary of the Sami does not include words for war, farming, or things unfamiliar to them. When it comes to nature, though, they are not lacking: eight seasons and 90 variations of snow conditions exist in their vocabulary!

This Sami woman from Finnmark is likely to speak Norwegian and her Sami dialect.

GUSTAV VIGELAND

1869 — 1943

ARTS

NORWAY HAS A LONG TRADITION in the arts—descending from the poems and legends of Viking times through Danish influence during Danish rule to the nationalist concerns of modern times. Among the oldest artistic works in Norway are the intricate wood carvings with which the Vikings decorated ships, buildings, wagons, sleighs, swords, and many other objects.

SCULPTURE

The first Norwegian sculptor to win international fame, Gustav Vigeland (1869–1943), has an entire park in Oslo dedicated to him. Vigeland Museum, which has Vigeland's ashes and many of his works, is also located in Vigeland Park. In the 1920s the municipality of Oslo offered Vigeland this building for his studio and residence. In return, he donated all his works to the city.

Vigeland Park was designed by Vigeland himself. The park exhibits many of his best works, whose main theme is the various phases of human life, from infancy to old age. Many of his sculptures represent scenes from everyday life. In *Angry Boy*, Vigeland immortalized a young boy throwing a tantrum. The work that most people see as the park's main masterpiece is *The Monolith*, a sculpture 55 feet (17 m) tall, representing 121 humans struggling toward a summit. Vigeland Park, which also features a sculpted self-portrait of Vigeland, draws over one million visitors a year.

Above: **A Viking ship from the Viking Ship Museum in Oslo.**

Opposite: **A sculpted self-portrait of Gustav Vigeland in Vigeland Park.**

Ladies on the Quay departs from the themes of death and despair that characterize many paintings by Edvard Munch.

PAINTING

The nationalistic movement in literature that arose in the 19th century influenced the visual arts. Paintings of Norwegian landscapes and scenes of daily life replaced visual arts with Christian and Viking themes. Johan Christian Dahl (1788–1857) was at the forefront of the development of a Norwegian style of painting. Dahl introduced the mountain as a symbol that would recur in the works of later artists and writers. He taught in Dresden, Germany.

EDVARD MUNCH   Norway's best-known artist is Edvard Munch (1863–1944). Munch's ability to portray the trauma of modern psychic life through distortion of colors and forms made him one of the most influential modern artists.

Munch, who came from an old Norwegian professional family, was greatly affected by the deaths of his mother when he was 5 years of age and his eldest sister when he was 14. Many critics feel that Munch's childhood explains the melancholy in his paintings. Munch himself said, in 1889, "No one should paint interiors anymore, people reading and women knitting. They should be living people who breathe and feel, suffer and love." His better-known works include *The Sick Child*, *Ashes*, *Death in the Room*, *Jealousy*, and *Summer Night*.

Munch gave his works to the city of Oslo, where they are now housed at the Munch Museum. In 1994 his best-known painting, *Skrik* (*The Scream* or *The Cry*), which he called a scream against nature, was stolen. It was recovered later that year but was stolen again in August 2004, along with Munch's *Madonna*. The Munch Museum was subsequently closed in a bid to revamp and beef up its security. Six suspects were scheduled for trial in 2006 for allegedly planning or carrying out the robbery, and it was hoped that some information about the whereabouts of the paintings might be revealed.

MUSIC

Norway has a long tradition of music that includes folk songs, fiddling, and brass bands. Just about every school has a marching band, which is where many of Norway's jazz musicians got their start.

Norway's most famous composer is Edvard Grieg (1843–1907). Grieg did not write symphonies, but he did take on large projects. He is world famous for writing the music for Henrik Ibsen's *Peer Gynt*. He is also known for his piano sonatas, 10 volumes of lyrical pieces inspired by the poems of Henrik Ibsen and Arne Garborg. Grieg, who also wrote Norwegian folk songs and music for Norwegian dances, is equally well known in Norway for a little rubber frog that he kept in his pocket. It is believed that by rubbing its rough-textured back before a concert he calmed his nerves. The frog is part of the permanent Grieg exhibit at the composer's home.

Modern composer Arne Nordheim (born in 1931) took Norwegian classical music by storm two generations after Grieg's death. He produces experimental works, often combining orchestral music with taped electronically processed acoustic sounds.

Edvard Grieg's compositions were stamped with the mark of his Norwegian heritage.

When Knut Hamsun visited the United States in 1886, he worked on farms in the Midwest and as a streetcar conductor in Chicago. He also gave lectures on modern European writers in Minneapolis.

LITERATURE

Norwegian Vikings who settled in Iceland orally passed on their beliefs, history, and myths through stories. These were written down in the 13th century *Eddas*, books that tell of the various mythical gods and heroes of Scandinavia.

The first important writer of the modern period was Henrik Wergeland (1808–45). He wrote love and nature poems and numerous essays. He established a free personal lending library. A devout nationalist, Wergeland called upon Norwegians to free themselves of Danish influence, and he set up a school in his own home where he taught Norwegian. He set the pattern for creative writers to be public advocates for democracy and freedom.

Wergeland's sister Camilla Collett (1813–95) wrote Norway's first feminist novel, *The Governor's Daughter*—the first part published in 1854 and the second in 1855—decrying the position of women forced into marriage. Collett inspired other female writers, including Amalie Skram (1847–1905) who, in her novels *Constance Ring* and *Betrayed*, continued Collett's theme of disastrous marriages.

Around the beginning of the 20th century, Norwegian writers focused on the struggles of the individual. Many 20th-century novels explore social problems and feature protagonists who reject modern society. In 1920 Knut Hamsun (1859–1952), best known for his novels *Hunger* and *Growth of the Sun*, was awarded the Nobel Prize in literature.

HENRIK IBSEN

The work of Henrik Ibsen (1828–1906) revolutionized theater. His plays aroused enormous criticism, but people flocked to see them. James Joyce, the great Irish writer, was so enamored of Ibsen's plays that he taught himself Norwegian in order to study them. A strong supporter of women's rights, Ibsen is known for creating many great female characters, such as Nora in *A Doll's House*, which is about women's liberation and the hypocrisy of marriage.

Ibsen's major plays are set in Norway, with a recognizably Norwegian landscape, but his characters and themes have universal significance. Ibsen portrayed people as they are; his characters struggle with problems that society of their time was afraid to mention, such as marital discord and illegitimacy. Over the course of 50 years, Ibsen published 25 plays and a volume of poetry.

SIGRID UNDSET, THE NOBEL LAUREATE

In 1928 another Norwegian writer, Sigrid Undset (1882–1949), was awarded the Nobel Prize in literature for her long historical novel *Kristin Lavransdatter*, set in 13th-century Norway. Undset, considered to be Norway's greatest woman writer, was taught the Old Norse sagas and Scandinavian folk songs at an early age by her archaeologist father. Although Undset is not regarded as a feminist, her novels provide insight into women's lives not found elsewhere in Norwegian fiction. Her early novels centered on the lives of ordinary working women and how they dealt with conflicts between personal needs and ambitions and family responsibilities.

During the 1930s Undset wrote vehemently against the rise of Nazism in Germany, which put her on the Nazis' most-wanted list. When the Nazis occupied Norway, Undset escaped to Sweden, then made her way across Siberia to Japan, and then to the United States. She spent the war years actively working for the Norwegian government in exile. After the war, she returned to her home in Lillehammer and died four years later.

"I would rather play Ibsen than eat," declared American actress Eva Le Gallienne (1899–1991), who translated and acted in many of Ibsen's plays.

The National Theater in Oslo was opened in 1899. In the late 1960s theaters in Olso, Bergen, Stavanger, and Trondheim underwent expansions and started subsidiary theaters. This doubled the production of plays and helped the boom in drama and the performing arts that Norway has experienced since the late 1970s.

DRAMA

By European standards, Norway's theater traditions are very young. Professional theater began only in 1827, when Swedish Johan Peter Strømberg opened his theater in Oslo. Norway's oldest existing theater is the National Stage in Bergen, which was opened in 1876.

Henrik Ibsen, Norway's most famous playwright, well-known all over the world for plays such as *Peer Gynt* and *A Doll's House*, is acknowledged as the father of modern Norwegian drama. Norway also had another prominent playwright, Nordahl Grieg, who wrote plays that dealt with the human psyche and questioned one's inner self.

The National Traveling Theater, or Riksteatret (riks-teh-AH-ter-eht), was founded in 1948, using the Swedish Riksteatret as its model. The Riksteatret takes professional drama all over Norway, to towns and villages that would otherwise be deprived as they are too small to support their own theater companies. It is the equivalent of the circus coming to town, and no one who can help it will miss a performance of the Riksteatret.

Permanent theaters are awarded grants by government, county, and local authorities that cover almost 90 percent of their operating expenses.

MOVIES

Most Norwegian movie theaters show foreign films, mainly from the United States and Europe. The Norwegian movie industry is still in its early stages, although it is starting to make a name for itself. Some Norwegian movies have crossed the Atlantic, such as Arne Schouen's *Gategutter* (*Street Boys*) and *Ni Liv* (*Nine Lives*), which was nominated for an Academy Award in 1957.

The early 1980s saw the Norwegian movie industry dominated by women directors like Vibeke Løkkeberg, Anja Breien, and Bente Erichsen, but in the late 1980s male directors caught up with successful action movies. In 1986 Oddvar Einarson's movie *X* was awarded the judges' special prize in the Venice film festival.

Perhaps the best-known Norwegian movie is Nils Gaup's *Veiviseren* (*Pathfinder*), which was nominated for an Academy Award for Best Foreign Film in 1988. *Veiviseren* is based on Sami folklore from the Middle Ages. This marked a new chapter in the Norwegian movie industry with more Norwegian movies achieving international acclaim. In 2003 more films were released than in any previous year.

In the big cities, going to the movies is a regular affair. However, many of the smaller towns do not have a movie theater. For residents of these towns, going to a movie is a real night out, as they have to drive to the nearest large town or city. Often they will get together with a couple of friends, have dinner first, and then make their way to the town in time for the movie.

The Borgund stave church in Sogn.

STAVKIRKER *ARCHITECTURE*

Norway's rich tradition in wood carving is documented in stories from the medieval period when carpentry was a craft entrusted only to men of rank. When Norway was converted to Christianity, Norwegians developed their own form of religious architecture in the *stavkirker* (stahv-KHEER-ker), or stave churches, which are thought to be quintessentially Norwegian. Norway had over 1,000 of these wooden churches in the medieval period. Only about 30 remain intact.

No nails were used in the construction of stave churches. Norwegian pine wood was measured and cut precise lengths to form planks, columns and beams, then pieced together. Stave churches were also traditionally raised above ground level to preserve the wooden structure from rotting.

The stave churches retained Viking design elements and also displayed Christian influences from other parts of Europe. These churches were small, dark, and plain, without pews or pulpits. The most distinctive art works could be found at the doorframe where animals and intertwining lines, similar to Viking wood carvings, decorated the doors, especially the large west doors that served as the main entrance.

SAMI ARTISTIC TRADITIONS

FOLK DRESS The only district where folk dress is still worn daily as well as for holidays is Samiland. In the winter the Sami who inhabit the area that used to be Lappland wear fur on their heads and bodies, right to their feet, but in the summer they wear their most colorful traditional clothing. This has fabric patterned with delicate embroidery around the throat and shoulders. Samis often wear beautiful belts woven in bright colors.

THE JOIK An old Sami form of musical expression is the *joik* (yoy-IK), a type of yodeling. Traditionally, the *joik* imitates animals, such as the wolf, reindeer, or long-tailed duck. A *joik* can also tell an ancient Sami myth or serve as a commentary on current events. The most popular forms of *joik* are character sketches of individuals that can be changed as the person changes. A Sami does not write his or her own *joik*, and once one is written about a person, it is customary to regard it as belonging to that person. The memory of deceased persons is kept alive by reciting their *joik*.

In traditional religious ceremonies the *joik* was used to help the shaman—a religious figure who performs a priestlike role—enter a trance while beating a drum. During the Norwegianization process, the *joik* and drumming were outlawed. Today, Sami revivalization has evoked a renewed interest in the *joik* tradition, and it has acquired value as an important cultural symbol. In recent years one *joik* made it to the top of the Norwegian hit parade.

LEISURE

SKIING IS A NORWEGIAN passion, a natural consequence of the climate and terrain of the country. Skiing is not a recent invention. A 4,000-year-old rock carving in Nordland near the Arctic Circle shows a person on two skis. Skis about 2,300 years old have been found preserved in bogs. Old Norse mythology had both a ski god (Ull) and a ski goddess (Skade).

Soccer is very popular in Norway, as it is in most other parts of the world. Also enjoyed are boating, fishing, rowing, swimming, hiking and cycling.

A NATION OF SKIERS

Almost every Norwegian owns a pair of skis. Norwegians take their first skiing lessons at age 2 or 3. Schoolchildren look forward to ski days and ski vacations, and adults often go off on ski runs to unwind after a hard day at work. After dusk, adults ski the many miles of lighted trails through woods wearing a cap with a light, similar to a miner's cap. Those feeling deprived during the summer often pack their skis and make their way to the glaciers of Jotunheimen National Park.

Norway is known as the home of modern skiing. Sondre Norheim (1825–97), a poor farmer from Morgedal in the Telemark region, devised a ski that was narrower in the middle and had stiff bindings around the heel. This was called the Telemark ski, and it enabled Norheim to execute jumps and turns without losing his skis, earning him the title of "father of modern skiing."

Above: **There is a saying that Norwegians are born with skis on their feet. Certainly, they are taught to ski at a very young age.**

Opposite: **A Norwegian family enjoying ice climbing together.**

Norwegians excel at speed skating, and their athletes carry away prizes at every Winter Olympics. Here, Norwegian silver medalist Kjell Storelid goes through his paces at Lillehammer in 1994.

Norheim and some other ski enthusiasts soon became known for their daring feats. They entered competitions where they could demonstrate their techniques. Norheim was 50 when he retired from competitions, but he taught his techniques to children. Later he went to the United States, where others from Telemark had introduced skiing.

The first recorded skiing competitions with prizes in Norway date from 1866. By 1903 foreigners were taking part in the annual competitions. With the popularity of skiing as a sport instead of simply as a form of transportation, hotels that previously closed for the winter discovered they could now stay open all year round. In 1924 the first Winter Olympics were held in Chamonix, France, with Norwegians taking the top four spots in the 31-mile (50-km) race. In the 2006 Winter Olympics in Torino, Italy, Norway won 19 medals, including Kjetil Andre Aamodt's third straight gold medal for skiing the Super-G. In the end, Norway's ranking among the 85 participating nations was 13th.

ICE SKATING

The first speed-skating contest in Norway was held on the ice in a fjord near Oslo's Akershus Fortress in 1885. In the 1950s speed-skating champions were national heroes. Since then, interest in the sport has diminished, although in 1991 Norway gained a new national hero in Johan Koss, who made sports history when he broke three world records during the world speed-skating championships in the Netherlands, followed by winning a gold medal at the 1994 Winter Olympics.

In figure skating, Sonja Henie, Norway's darling of the 1920s, brought fame to Norway as the world's figure-skating champion at age 15. She retained the title for 10 years and won the Olympic gold medal three times. In Hollywood she starred in many popular movies during the late 1930s and early 1940s.

WOMEN IN SPORTS

Although Norwegian women today are winning many of the top spots in international sporting events such as marathons, handball, and soccer, it has been only recently that female athletes were fully accepted in Norway. In 1888 Lillehammer sponsored the world's first ski races for women, but it is only since the 1960s that Norwegian women have been taken seriously in cross-country skiing competitions.

The acceptance of sportswomen in Norway is attributed to Grete Waitz (born in 1953), who won the New York marathon nine times out of 10 races between 1978 and 1988. She started a run through the streets of Oslo in 1982, and it has since become an annual event.

In 1927, at the World Figure-Skating Championship in Oslo, Sonja Henie (*above*) took first place, beating Hanna Planck-Szabo of Austria. The decision was mired in controversy, however, because all three Norwegian judges voted for Henie, whereas the Austrian and German judges gave higher marks to Planck-Szabo. After that, no country has had more than one judge on a panel.

SPORTS FOR THE PHYSICALLY CHALLENGED

In 1964 Erling Stordahl, who was blind, arranged the first ski race in Norway, the Ridderrennet, for the visually handicapped, using deeper ski trails and a guiding system of beeping sounds along the trail. Today disabled athletes can participate in their respective sports alongside able-bodied athletes. This follows a historic decision in 1996 by the Norwegian Confederation of Sports to fully integrate sports for everyone, able-bodied or not. Upon his demise in Norway in 1994, a state funeral was held for Erling in honor of his passion for and contributions to the disabled and visually impaired.

A family goes mountain hiking in Telemark.

NO FENCES

Norway's grand and beautiful wilderness areas, which have inspired artists and musicians, are accessible to everyone in Norway. Norwegians spend much of their free time hiking, skiing, fishing, cycling, and mountain climbing. In fact, the reluctance of Oslo residents to leave the city—it lies in the middle of the Nordmarka forest area—because they are so fond of walks through the woods is referred to as the Nordmarka syndrome. The Norwegian Mountain Touring Association, the oldest organization of its kind in the world, marks trails and rents out cabins for overnight accommodation to help hikers.

The right of access to uncultivated areas is very important in Norway. Fortunately, along with free access, most Norwegians are conscious of their obligations. They know they may not walk about in newly planted forest; break off, cut, or in any way damage plants; disturb animals and birds, including their nests and young; or trample fields and meadows.

INKY Norwegian children are encouraged to enjoy the outdoors from a very early age. Along with a love for nature, they are very conscious of environmental issues. When she was a child, Norwegian Bente Roestad saw an octopus for the first time while living in Greece. Years later, she created stories about the octopus, which she called Inky, for her 5-year-old nephew. The simple stories about the wise blue octopus grew into a series of books and later a television series about the threat of pollution to marine life. The shows provoked 40,000 calls from children who wanted to know how they could help, and the Norwegian Society for the Conservation of Nature started the Inky Club for children aged 5 to 13. Its members call in to radio shows, expose environmental misdemeanors, and write articles for newspapers. One such environmental "detective," Bjørn Carlsen, age 13, discovered that industrial waste was seeping from a landfill into a children's play area and also polluting a nearby lake.

Long-distance cyclists take the precaution of wearing helmets in case of spills or accidents.

Like the Vikings, many Norwegians today have a keen sense of adventure and are avid sailors.

EXPLORERS

Harking back to the traditional occupation of their Viking ancestors as daring explorers who set sail for parts unknown, several Norwegians have attempted grueling expeditions to far reaches of the earth. They include Fridtjof Nansen, Otto Sverdrup, Roald Amundsen, Thor Heyerdahl, Ragnar Thorseth, and, most recently, Liv Arnesen.

FRIDTJOF NANSEN Before he became a delegate to the League of Nations, Fridtjof Nansen was a well-known scientist. To prove his hypothesis that the Arctic current flowed from Siberia toward the North Pole and then down to Greenland, Fridtjof Nansen designed a boat, the *Fram,* that would not break apart under the enormous pressure of ice. Together with 13 crew members, he headed east in July 1893.

Off the northeast coast of Siberia, the *Fram* was frozen into the ice pack. With knowledge gained from years of study, Nansen knew the boat would not pass over the North Pole. With a companion, three light sleds, 28 dogs, three kayaks, and food for 100 days, he set out in March 1895 for the North Pole.

By early April, Nansen realized they would not make it to the North Pole, although he had gone farther than any previous explorer. They then attempted to journey to Franz Joseph Land, 400 miles (640 km) to the southwest. In August they reached an uninhabited island north of Franz Joseph Land. As winter was closing in, they dug a three-foot hollow, made a roof of walrus skins, and sat out the nine-month winter.

In June 1896 they made it to one of the southern islands, where they encountered the English explorer Frederick Jackson, who had been commissioned to find an overland route to the North Pole. Nansen returned to Norway on Jackson's ship to a hero's welcome. A week later the *Fram* arrived in Norway, having drifted from Siberia to Svalbard, proving Nansen's theory true.

OTTO SVERDRUP The captain of the *Fram* for Nansen's drift expedition, Otto Sverdrup (1854–1930), took the *Fram* on a second expedition to the Arctic islands north of Canada and spent four years charting unexplored territory. Between 1910 and 1920 he led other polar expeditions. His maps were a valuable resource for explorers who came after him.

ROALD AMUNDSEN Like Fridtjof Nansen, Roald Amundsen (1872–1928) was a professional expeditioner who knew that courage without a lot of planning achieved little. Amundsen realized that success for an Arctic expedition meant combining the roles of scientist and navigator. In preparation, he not only trained physically by playing soccer, skiing, and

During his first voyage, Roald Amundsen *(above)* and his crew spent a summer and two winters doing research on King William Island. From the Netsilik Inuit people, Amundsen learned the value of pacing oneself. The Inuit know that sweat can kill a person in the Arctic, as well as be exhausting so that one cannot expend a burst of energy in an emergency. These lessons stood Amundsen in good stead for his later expedition to the South Pole.

Liv Arnesen, a 41-year-old Norwegian, became the first woman to reach the South Pole alone when she arrived there on Christmas Day in 1994 after skiing 746 miles (1,200 km) in 50 days.

sleeping with the window open in the winter, but also studied navigation and the theories of magnetism.

Amundsen wanted to be the first to navigate the so-called Northwest Passage. In the previous 400 years, 50 or 60 expeditions had been launched without success. In 1903, with a crew of six, Amundsen set out to find and navigate the Northwest Passage in a 31-year-old small herring boat. He was convinced the smallness of his vessel and patience would get him farther than the others, who had used much larger boats.

Amundsen was right. He got through the entire Northwest Passage, including a shallow island-dotted strait never before navigated. He wrote later that "it was just like sailing through an uncleared field." If he had been in a larger boat, he would not have succeeded.

PLANTING THE NORWEGIAN FLAG AT THE SOUTH POLE

After months of preparation, Roald Amundsen was just about to set out in Nansen's *Fram* for the North Pole when news that American Robert Peary had reached it reverberated around the world. Amundsen immediately changed his course for Antarctica and the South Pole, determined to reach it ahead of the British expedition headed by Robert Scott.

At the Bay of Whales in the Ross Sea, Amundsen set out overland with four men and 52 dogs. One of the four men was Olav Bjaaland, a skiing champion from Morgedal, who was given the task of making sure the skis and sleds were in top condition all the time. On December 14, 1911, the Norwegian group reached the South Pole and planted the Norwegian flag on King Haakon VII's Plateau. This was the expedition that made Roald Amundsen a household name around the world. Five weeks later, Robert Scott arrived at the pole to find the Norwegian flag and Amundsen's tent.

Amundsen died in 1928 while attempting to rescue Umberto Nobile, an explorer whose airship had crashed while attempting to fly over the North Pole. At a memorial service for Amundsen, who was buried in the Arctic, Fridtjof Nansen said that Amundsen had "returned to the expanses of the Arctic Ocean, where his life's work lay."

THOR HEYERDAHL Perhaps the best-known explorer of the 20th century, Thor Heyerdahl (1914–2000) did not follow in the footsteps of Nansen or Amundsen by exploring unchartered territories. Anthropology was his interest.

As a zoology and geography student, he traveled in 1937 to Polynesia to conduct research on animal life in the valleys of the island of Fatu-Hiva. Accepting anthropological theories that ancestors of the Polynesians had sailed there from Asia, Heyerdahl noticed something different that contradicted the theories: the people had much in common with South Americans in food, statues, and myths.

Thor Heyerdahl *(above)* sailed his reed boats under the United Nations flag with a multinational crew to show that peaceful coexistence, even under extreme conditions, is possible.

To prove the scientists who argued that South Americans could not have reached Polynesia in their primitive vessels wrong, Heyerdahl launched his famous Kon Tiki expedition. In 1947 he built a raft in the style of the Incas—a log raft held together by ropes and wooden pegs—and set out from Peru with five companions. In 101 days, having covered 5,000 miles (8,045 km), he reached the Raroia Atoll in Polynesia. He did not prove that the Polynesians' ancestors came from South America, but Heyerdahl proved it was possible.

Heyerdahl later made many other voyages in replicas of prehistoric boats. He traveled on papyrus reed boats, named *Ra I* and *Ra II*, from North Africa to the Caribbean in 1969 and 1970. In 1978 he sailed from the Middle East to East Asia and back to Africa in an Iraqi reed boat. All of Heyerdahl's voyages attempted to show the links between major early civilizations. Heyerdahl believed that the world's oceans have served as highways for humankind since the first boats were built.

FESTIVALS

NORWAY HAS FESTIVALS OF Christian origin, such as Christmas and Easter, and others of pre-Christian times that have been converted into either Christian or secular festivals, such as Midsummer's Day. Norwegians also celebrate international holidays, such as Labor Day, as well as national or local festivals, such as their Constitution Day and *russ* (rewss) celebrations.

Norwegians work hard in the course of the year, so they really let their hair down and celebrate on festival days. The streets are filled with people, and in the cities and towns it looks like one big party.

Labor Day in Europe has traditionally been a day for workers to demand better working conditions, increased benefits, and shorter working hours. However, in Norway, many feel there is little left to demand, with workers entitled to four weeks' paid vacation, two and a half days at Christmas, a minimum of five days at Easter, and the additional holidays of Ascension Day, Whitsuntide Monday, Labor Day, and Constitution Day, plus sick days for oneself or one's children and paid maternity and paternity leave. So Labor Day is enjoyed as a holiday.

Other holidays include the Holmenkollen Ski Festival, the Bergen Concert and Theater Festival at the end of May, and an international jazz week in Molde at the end of July. Early fall brings the international Ibsen Festival in Oslo, and December 10 is the day of the Nobel Peace Prize ceremony, an Oslo event that garners international attention.

"We use our holidays to celebrate the sun. We celebrate the arrival of the sun, the summer solstice, we journey to the mountains in search of the sun, and on the day we miss it the most, because it is farthest away, we cheer ourselves with a grand Christmas feast."
—Thor Heyerdahl

Opposite: **Norwegians usually wear traditional clothing during festivals and important occasions, such as weddings. The** *bunad* **(BOO-nahd) is a beautifully embroidered traditional dress, and the embroidery varies with each district. Such clothes are costly and are handed down from generation to generation.**

NORWEGIAN HOLIDAYS

March/April	Easter	November 1	All Saints' Day
May 1	Labor Day	December 10	Nobel Peace
May 17	Constitution Day		Prize
	Children's Day	December 25	Christmas Day
June 23	Midsummer's Day	December 26	Boxing Day

"Now stands the flagpole bare behind Eidsvoll's budding trees. But in such an hour as this, we know what freedom is."

—Norwegian poet, Nordahl Grieg, on the Nazi ban on Constitution Day celebrations

May 17 is an occasion for parades with the Norwegian flag and, for a few, for wearing their *bunad*, **or traditional dress.**

CONSTITUTION DAY

Constitution Day is the Norwegian equivalent of the Fourth of July celebrations in the United States. It falls on May 17, the anniversary of the day in 1814 when Norway's elected National Assembly issued a constitution that declared an end to the 400-year union with Denmark.

Constitution Day has been celebrated in various ways over the decades. After independence in 1905, parades emphasized nationhood. During the Nazi occupation of World War II, Constitution Day celebrations were forbidden. In the decades since World War II, parades have emphasized democratic rights, freedom of the press, and constitutional government.

CHILDRENS' DAY

May 17 has also become Children's Day in Norway, and thousands of schoolchildren participate in processions with their school bands in cities, towns, and villages all over the country. The Oslo parade ends at the Royal Palace, where the royal family waves to the children from a balcony.

The day is marked by firecrackers set off at dawn, between 4 and 5 A.M. High school graduates drive around in cars decorated with flowers and branches, wearing their *russ* or graduation suits. For them, Constitution Day marks the beginning of a three-week celebration of the end of high school.

RUSS *CELEBRATIONS*

High school graduates celebrate their graduation in a unique style, wearing their *russ* costumes and engaging in a three-week-long celebration. The term *russ* originated from a Latin word that refers to those who were sent to the university to study. Most *russ* are so-called *rødrusser* (red *russ*), graduates in the arts and the sciences, while *blåruss* (blue *russ*) are those who graduated in business, and *svartruss* (black *russ*) is for those who focused on vocational subjects.

Russ students are allowed many liberties. They are permitted to make as much noise as they wish, early in the morning, late at night, or all day. They can spray silly jingles about their teachers on the pavements with washable paint, or screnade teachers in the early hours of the morning. They can have as much fun as they wish, provided they do not engage in acts of vandalism that destroy property or harm anyone.

Teachers are not the only targets of *russ* students. Neighbors may have a rude, but never insulting, jingle about them sprayed on the pavement in front of their house. They will be embarrassed by it, but it is all permitted and accepted in a spirit of fun.

Russ graduates in high spirits on a street in Oslo. Years ago, *russ* celebrations had a cultural emphasis, with graduates organizing plays and other performances. The cultural aspect is missing today.

Midsummer's Eve is the time for small barbecues near a big bonfire with sausages, fancy dress, and much gaiety. Mindful of fire hazards, parents spray the grass nearby with water before the bonfire is lit.

EASTER

Easter celebrations are less a religious occasion in Norway than a rejoicing in the lengthening of the days, a sign that summer is not too far away. In the north the Sami gather to celebrate weddings, confirmations, and baptisms, and all Norwegians who live north of the Arctic Circle celebrate the return of the sun after weeks of darkness.

Although many Norwegians spend the five-day Easter break with family and close friends, Easter is also a time for celebrating solitude and independence and communing with nature. Many Norwegians take off on solitary journeys and travel up into the mountains to do just that. A popular Easter joke tells of a Norwegian professor who, when asked how he had enjoyed his Easter holiday in the mountains, replied, "It was a total failure. I met somebody."

MIDSUMMER'S DAY

Midsummer, or the summer solstice, is the longest day of the year. Early Vikings often held their assemblies on Midsummer's Day, which was also allegedly the annual meeting day for witches. The feast of the bonfires on the summer solstice is one of the oldest celebrations in northern Europe. In Christian times the day was renamed Saint John's Eve, in honor of John the Baptist. Today heaps of wood are collected for days beforehand. On Midsummer's Eve, huge bonfires are lit, and the crowd drinks, eats, and dances all night long.

CHRISTMAS

Jul (yewl), or Christmas, is a busy time for churches, which hold special Advent services, and for households, as traditionally all the wood must be cut, cakes baked, food prepared, and beer brewed by December 21, Saint Thomas's Day. On Christmas Eve families sit down to a traditional Christmas dinner, which includes *pinnekjøtt* (PINE-shuht) and *gløgg* (gluhg). *Pinnekjøtt*, meaning twig meat, is salted lamb ribs, so named because a rack of birch twigs is placed in the bottom of the pan used to steam the ribs. *Gløgg*, descended from the Viking drink mead, is wine or juice mulled with raisins, ginger,

cardamom, cinnamon, and other spices, served warm. It is a favorite Christmas drink. After the meal the family walks around the Christmas tree singing traditional carols. Gifts are exchanged and opened and celebrations last for 20 days, until Saint Knut's Day, on January 13.

Norwegian families decorate their Christmas trees with white candles, a remnant of traditional midwinter bonfires. An almond ring cake, which takes a long time to prepare and is therefore usually served only on festive occasions, takes pride of place at the table. In the 18th century food was often left on the table from Christmas Eve to Epiphany (January 6). All who entered the house had to sample the food, for if they left without doing so they were thought to "carry Christmas out of the house."

THE GHOSTS OF CHRISTMAS

Before the idea of Santa Claus was imported into Norway by department stores hoping to increase their year-end sales, Christmas was a time associated with visits from ghosts. Norwegians believed their ancestors returned to their earthly homes in midwinter. Until the late 19th century, straw was left in many homes for the invisible "guests" to sleep on during the holiday season, and bread was left out for them to eat. In a popular fairy tale a family was regularly chased out of their home by an invading horde of Christmas ghosts. The ghosts were finally outwitted by a white bear, and they never returned.

FOOD

LIVING CLOSE TO the sea, Norwegians have historically depended on seafood for much of their diet. Cooks prepare fish in various ways, frequently serving it with boiled potatoes and vegetables during the main meal of the day, *middag* (mid-DAHG), which mostly takes place between 4 and 6 P.M. Norwegians eat three other meals—breakfast, lunch, and supper. Each meal features *smørbrød* (SMUHR-brur), open-faced sandwiches of bread or crackers layered with cheese, jam, salmon spread, boiled egg, tomato, cucumber, sausage, herring, or sardines.

Above: **Middag is the time when families sit down to eat together and share the events of their day.**

Opposite: **A man slicing salmon in a fish market in Norway.**

Some Norwegian delicacies are salty and have a strong odor. *Gravet* (grah-VUHT), or smoked salmon, is a favorite, and some Norwegians savor *rakørret* (RAHK-uhr-ruht), or trout aged for months until it has a soft, buttery consistency and a pungent odor. Lamb is the most common meat, and blood sausage—a mixture of blood and flour—is a national specialty.

Traditional desserts include fruit soups, *rømmegrøt* (RUH-muh-gruhrt), or sour cream porridge, and fresh berries during the summer.

SMØRGÅSBORD

Smørgåsbord (SMUHR-gaws-boor), a word that has entered the English vocabulary as "smorgasbord" means an overflowing buffet table and an opportunity to indulge oneself. *Smørgåsbord* is a Swedish word to describe the Scandinavian practice of laying out a buffet spread with a multitude of different dishes, from spicy cured herring and other fish to

123

Two female fish dealers pose proudly with their stock. Fresh, pickled, or in a mixture that is ready to cook in *fiskeboller*—fish varieties abound in the marketplace.

meats, salads, and cheeses. The term literally means "bread and butter table," and the idea is that one helps oneself to various dishes and eats them with bread and butter. The actual Norwegian (and Danish) name is *koldtbord* (KOLT-boor), which means cold table, but the Swedish word is better known and generally used. A ritual is attached to the smorgasbord. One must begin with the various cured herring, take a fresh plate for the meats and salads, and then finish up with cheese. The usual adult beverages served during a smorgasbord are schnapps, aquavit (AH-qeh-vit), and beer.

TYPICAL DISHES

Almost every Norwegian dish includes potatoes—sliced, boiled, fried, in stews, and in any other way imaginable. The potato has been a staple of the Norwegian diet since the early 19th century.

Norwegians eat a heavily meat- and fish-based diet. A children's favorite is *kjøttkaker* (shet-KAH-ker), or meatballs in brown sauce. Norwegians have been known to take canned *kjøttkaker* with them when traveling in case they do not get accustomed to the local food. *Fårikål* (fawr-EE-kawl) is a traditional thick, rich lamb stew cooked with cabbage. This is often made in the fall when lamb is abundant. *Fiskeboller* (fis-kuh-BOWL-cr), or Norwegian fishballs made from a mixture of fish, salt, and water, are an acquired taste. *Lapskaus* (lahps-KAH-oos), a meat and potato stew made with salted pork or leftover meats, is a thick, chunky stew popular with everyone.

Lutefisk (LEW-tuh-fisk), usually served a few weeks before Christmas, is most definitely an acquired taste. It is prepared by soaking dried cod in lye water for two or three days until the flesh is soft enough to poke a finger through. The cod is then soaked in running cold water for two days to remove all traces of lye, and then cut into large pieces and boiled or poached. *Lutefisk* is often served with *lefse* (LEHF-suh), or Norwegian flatbread, and can be eaten with peas or white sauce and mustard.

"Finnish beef" is not really beef at all, but a Sami speciality made from very thin slices of reindeer meat browned in butter and seasoned with salt and pepper. It is often served with some goat cheese, lingonberry jelly, and, of course, boiled or mashed potatoes.

MUSHROOM AND BERRY PICKING

More Norwegians are acquiring a taste for mushrooms. This increasing interest has developed into a pastime of nature walks combined with mushroom picking. Berry picking, on the other hand, has long been a leisure activity for the entire family. The rewards of both mushroom and berry picking include delicious dishes, jams, and pies.

Norway's vast forests are public domain, even if parts of them are owned by farmers. There is a right of public access to all forested areas

The potato arrived in Norway in the 18th century and was at first available only to government employees and the upper classes. The clergy soon realized the merits of this tuber and used their pulpits to spread the word, giving rise to the era of the potato preachers. Farmers were convinced, and a good thing too, because during the famine years, from 1804 to 1814, potatoes became the mainstay of the Norwegian diet, a position that the humble tuber has not relinquished.

A shopper can choose from a wide selection of Norwegian cheeses.

in Norway, and everyone is free to pick mushrooms or berries.

In late summer there are lush bushes full of wild raspberries just waiting to be made into scrumptious desserts. In the fall the mountains are bursting with other luscious berries, including blueberries, lingonberries (a tart, cranberrylike berry very popular in Norway and often made into jelly), and the less abundant tart tasting cloudberries, a Scandinavian delicacy.

CHEESE, ANYONE?

Norwegian cheeses include Gulost, Gamalost, and Pultost. The famous brands are Jarlsberg, Gudbrandsdal, and Ridder. Jarlsberg, popular in Norway, is also the best known outside of the country. Gudbrandsdal is cheese that is regarded as the most Norwegian. First made in the 1850s in Fron in the Gudbrandsdalen area, this red cheese is most popular at the Norwegian breakfast table due to its sweet, caramelized flavor. Gamalost means old cheese, and this sharp-flavored cheese is well named, both for its pungent odor and because it has roots going back to Viking times.

"FREIA!"

From hot chocolate to candy bars, chocolate is a Norwegian passion. Every Norwegian consumes, on average, 17.6 pounds (8 kg) of chocolate a year. Half of this is produced by Freia.

Freia is Norway's most famous chocolate factory, immortalized in Roald Dahl's enormously popular book and movie *Charlie and the Chocolate Factory*. Freia had its beginnings in 1892 when founder Johan Throne Holst, with his brother and brother-in-law, bought a small chocolate factory in the Rødelokka district in Oslo. Given its humble beginnings, Freia, which is still located in Rødelokka, is today one of Norway's success stories. One of every two chocolate bars sold in Norway is made by Freia, and the company also exports chocolates all over the world.

Freia markets different varieties of chocolate bars: Firkløver, with hazelnuts, is the snack bar for a mini pick-me-up during a busy day and KvikkLunsj, a chocolate-coated wafer, is the candy bar of choice for a hiking trip. Known outside Norway as "a little piece of Norway," Freia milk chocolate is smooth and rich.

Freia also gained the endorsement of famous Norwegian explorer Roald Amundsen, who stated after his return from his major South Pole expedition that Freia chocolate was one of his team's main sources of nourishment during the grueling journey.

COOKING WITH CREATIVITY

Norway is certainly not short of culinary talent. At the Bocuse d'Or, one of the most prestigious cooking competitions, held in Lyon, France, every two years, Norwegian chefs have consistently been winners. In recent years Norwegian food has been experiencing a renaissance with a new, young generation of chefs fusing Norwegian traditions with contemporary, Continental styles. One such chef is Andreas Viestad, Norway's culinary ambassador, who has been in the forefront in promoting this new style of Scandinavian cooking. The result of this renaissance in cooking is refreshingly creative menus that showcase the best Norwegian ingredients.

Freia is a company with a social conscience. Promoting Norwegian culture and arts has become an inherent part of the company's mission. In 1920 Freia created the Freia Park, one of Oslo's finest parks, exhibiting the works of European sculptors, including Norwegian Gustav Vigeland. In 1922 Freia invited Norwegian artist Edvard Munch to decorate its employees' lunchroom. And in 1934 Freia Hall, home of the Oslo Philharmonic Orchestra, was opened.

BEER AND WINE

Beer drinking is a Scandinavian tradition. During Viking times and the Middle Ages, beer was served at formal occasions. Whether it is to make an agreement legally binding or to celebrate the baptism of an infant or a wedding, beer is served. As the price of beer is high in Norway, many Norwegians brew their own beer in the basements of their homes.

Wine is also popular, but as Norway's climate is unsuitable for grape cultivation, Norwegians make wine from other fruits and from flowers. Wine making is a popular hobby. Fruit and flower wines must be aged for a year but, with their refreshing taste, are well worth the wait.

Norwegians enjoying a cool beverage in the summertime.

COFFEE

Traders brought coffee to Norway about 250 years ago, but as it was both foreign and expensive, only the wealthy consumed it. Modern Norwegians have made up for lost time with a vengeance. Norwegians consume an average of 12.25 pounds (5.4 kg) per person, making them the world's biggest consumers of coffee per inhabitant. And they are coffee purists who prefer to drink their coffee black to savor its full aroma and flavor. Guests are usually served coffee with cakes or *smørbrød*.

AQUAVIT—THE NATIONAL DRINK

Aquavit, known as a Scandinavia's cross-national drink and for its contribution to the world's array of liquors, was first sold in the 16th century as a medicinal potion. Eske Bille, who created the drink in 1531, named it Aqua Vitæ (water of life), "a cure for all ills," and over the years this liquor graduated from medicinal potion to social beverage. Aquavit is made from potatoes and flavored with orange peel and several spices, including anise, fennel, caraway, and coriander. Aquavit is traditionally served with appetizers but it can also be served as an after-dinner drink.

The best-known aquavit in Europe is Linie Aquavit, or line aquavit, so called because the aquavit has passed over the equator. Many years ago, ships setting out from Trøndelag carried Norwegian aquavit on board as an export product. Not all the aquavit was sold, and when sampling the remainder, people noticed that the long journey had given the aquavit a new, enticing aroma. Since 1850, aquavit has been aged in oak vats on ships plying the route between Norway and Australia. Every bottle of aquavit has the name of the ship it was aged aboard, where it has been, and the duration of the journey recorded on its label.

KJØTTKAKER (NORWEGIAN MEATBALLS)

Meatballs:
4 slices white bread
¾ cup hot skim milk
1 pound (450 g) extra-lean
ground beef
½ pound (175 g) lean
ground pork
2 eggs, beaten
¼ teaspoon nutmeg
¼ teaspoon pepper
⅛ teaspoon allspice
½ cup chopped onion
2 teaspoons salt
2 teaspoons vegetable oil

Gravy:
4 tablespoons butter
4 tablespoons all-purpose flour
2 teaspoons beef bouillon
2½ cups boiling water

Preheat the oven to 350°F (175°C). Soak the bread in hot milk in a large mixing bowl until the milk is absorbed. Add all remaining meatball ingredients and mix well. Shape mixture into meatballs, each of a diameter of 1 inch (2.5 cm). Heat oil in a pan and fry meatballs until evenly browned. Drain oil and arrange the meatballs in a large casserole dish.

To make the gravy, melt the butter in a medium-sized saucepan. Stir in the flour. Mix bouillon into the boiling water and add this to the flour mixture. Cook and stir the mixture until it is thickened. Pour the gravy over the meatballs and bake the dish for 30 minutes. Serve the *kjøttkaker* over cooked rice or noodles. Makes six servings.

STRAWBERRY CAKE ROLL

2 eggs
$\frac{1}{3}$ cup whole milk
1 teaspoon sugar
$3\frac{1}{2}$ tablespoons flour
2 tablespoons melted butter
$1\frac{1}{4}$ cups strawberries
sugar
confectioner's sugar

Separate the eggs. In a large mixing bowl, use a whisk to beat the egg yolks, milk, sugar, and flour together until a smooth mixture is formed. In a separate bowl, beat the egg whites until they are stiff. Fold the egg whites into the first mixture. Brush a large, nonstick frying pan with melted butter over low heat. Pour in the batter and cover the pan. Cook the batter for approximately 10 minutes. Set the cake aside for it to cool. Slice the strawberries and mix the slices with sugar. Spoon the sugared strawberries over the cake and then roll it up. Dust the cake roll with confectioner's sugar, and then serve it with berries, whipped cream, or ice cream. Makes one serving.

MAP OF NORWAY

Akershus, B4
Åltaelv, D1
Arctic Circle, D2
Atlantic Ocean, A3
Austagder, B5

Baltic Sea, C5
Barents Sea, D1
Bergen, A4
Bodø, C2
Boknfjord, A4
Buskerud, B4

Denmark, A5, B5
Dovrefjell, B4
Drammen, B4
Dramselva, B4

Edgeøya, A1
Eidsvoll, B4
Elverum, B4

Finland, C1, C2,
  D1–D4
Finnmark, D1
Finnmarksvidda, D1
Fredrikstad, B5

Galdhøpiggen, A4
Glåma, B4
Glittertind, B4
Gudbrandsdalen, B4

Hallingdal, B4
Hamar, B4
Hammerfest, D1
Hardangerfjord, A4
Hardangervidda, A4
Haugesund, A4
Hedmark, B4
Hordaland, A4

Jæren Dalene, A4
Jan Mayen, A2
Jostedalsbreen, A4
Jotunheimen,
  A4, B4

Karasjok, D1
Kautokeino, D2
Kristiansand, A5

Lågen, B4
Langfjellene, C2
Lillehammer, B4
Lofoten islands, B2

Magerøya, D1
Mjøsa, Lake, B4
Mo i Rana, C2
Møre og Romsdal, B3

Namsen, B3
Narvik, C2
Nord-Jan, A2

NordTrøndelag, B3
Nordaustlandet, A1
Nordland, C2
North Atlantic
  Ocean, A3
North Sea, A5, B5
Norwegian Sea, B1

Oppland, B4
Orkla, B3
Oslo, B4
Oslofjord, B5
Otra, A5

Rogaland, A4
Røros, B4

Skagerrak, A5
Skien, B5
Sogn og Fjordane,
  A4

Sognefjord, A4
Sør-Jan, A2
Sørtrøndelag, B3
Spitsbergen, A1
Stavanger, A5
Svalbard, A1
Sweden, B3–B5,
  C1–C5, D2, D3

Tana, D1
Telemark, B4
Troms, C1
Tromsø, C1
Trondheim, B3
Trondheimfjord, B3

Vadsø, D1
Varsø, D1
Vestagder, A5
Vesterålen, C2
Vestfo, B5

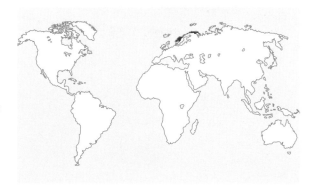

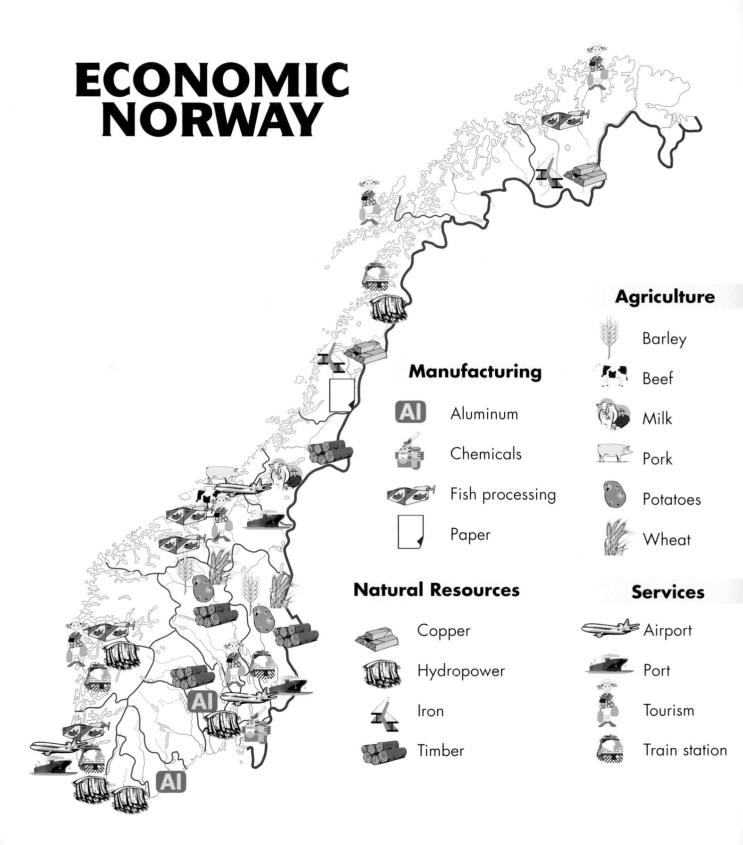

ECONOMIC NORWAY

Manufacturing

Al	Aluminum
	Chemicals
	Fish processing
	Paper

Natural Resources

	Copper
	Hydropower
	Iron
	Timber

Agriculture

	Barley
	Beef
	Milk
	Pork
	Potatoes
	Wheat

Services

	Airport
	Port
	Tourism
	Train station

ABOUT
THE ECONOMY

OVERVIEW

Norway has experienced an economic shift from more traditional labor-intensive industries to the service sector. While oil and gas still account for the main contribution to Norway's wealth, most of the country's workforce are now employed in the service sector, with export of services exceeding export of goods in recent years.

POPULATION

4.6 million (2006 estimate)

GROSS DOMESTIC PRODUCT

$194.7 billion (2005 estimate)

GDP GROWTH

3.8 percent (2005 estimate)

INFLATION RATE

2.1 percent (2005 estimate)

EXTERNAL DEBT

$281 billion (Norway is a net external creditor) (2005 estimate)

CURRENCY

1 Norwegian krone (NOK) = 100 øre
Notes: 50, 100, 200, 500, 1,000 kroner
Coins: 50 øre, 1 krone, and 5, 10, and 20 kroner
1 USD = 6.76 NOK (February 2006)

NATURAL RESOURCES

Petroleum, natural gas, iron ore, copper, lead, zinc, titanium, pyrites, nickel, fish, timber, hydropower

AGRICULTURAL PRODUCTS

Barley, wheat, pork, beef, veal, milk, fish, potaotes

MAJOR EXPORTS

Petroleum and petroleum products, machinery and equipment, metals, chemicals, ships, fish (2004 estimate)

MAJOR IMPORTS

Machinery and equipment, chemicals, metals, foodstuffs (2004 estimate)

MAIN TRADE PARTNERS

Sweden, Germany, France, Denmark, UK, Netherlands, United States, China, Japan (2004 estimate)

WORKFORCE

2.4 million (2005 estimate)

UNEMPLOYMENT RATE

4.2 percent (2005 estimate)

AIRPORTS

100; 67 with paved runways; 33 with unpaved runways (2005 estimate)

INTERNET USERS

2.29 million (2002 estimate)

CULTURAL NORWAY

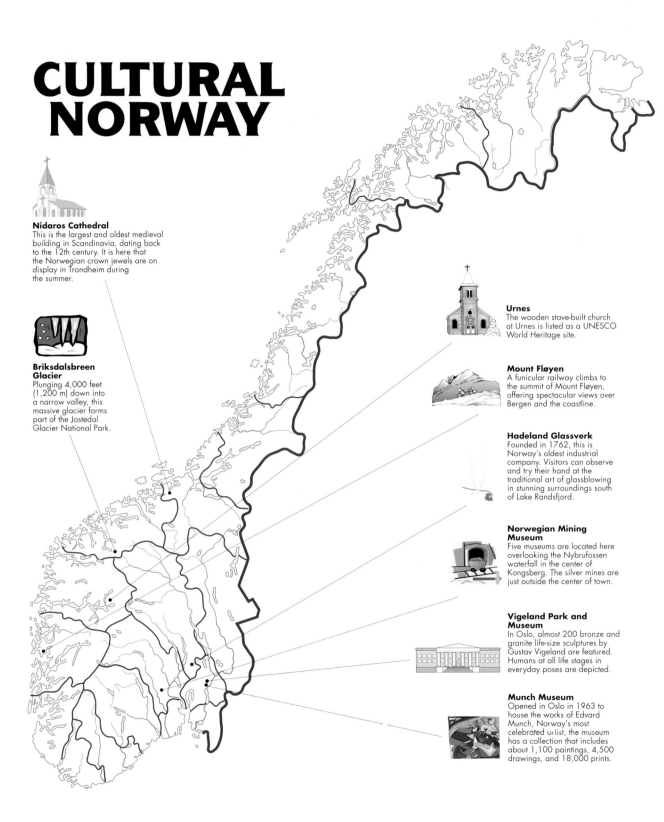

Nidaros Cathedral
This is the largest and oldest medieval building in Scandinavia, dating back to the 12th century. It is here that the Norwegian crown jewels are on display in Trondheim during the summer.

Briksdalsbreen Glacier
Plunging 4,000 feet (1,200 m) down into a narrow valley, this massive glacier forms part of the Jostedal Glacier National Park.

Urnes
The wooden stave-built church at Urnes is listed as a UNESCO World Heritage site.

Mount Fløyen
A funicular railway climbs to the summit of Mount Fløyen, offering spectacular views over Bergen and the coastline.

Hadeland Glassverk
Founded in 1762, this is Norway's oldest industrial company. Visitors can observe and try their hand at the traditional art of glassblowing in stunning surroundings south of Lake Randsfjord.

Norwegian Mining Museum
Five museums are located here overlooking the Nybrufossen waterfall in the center of Kongsberg. The silver mines are just outside the center of town.

Vigeland Park and Museum
In Oslo, almost 200 bronze and granite life-size sculptures by Gustav Vigeland are featured. Humans at all life stages in everyday poses are depicted.

Munch Museum
Opened in Oslo in 1963 to house the works of Edvard Munch, Norway's most celebrated artist, the museum has a collection that includes about 1,100 paintings, 4,500 drawings, and 18,000 prints.

ABOUT THE CULTURE

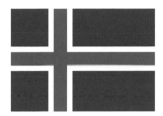

OFFICIAL NAME
Kingdom of Norway, Kongeriket Norge (in Norwegian)

CAPITAL
Oslo

NATIONAL FLAG
Red with a blue cross outlined in white that extends to the edges of the flag; the vertical part of the cross is shifted to the hoist side, very much like the Dannebrog (Danish flag).

TOTAL AREA
Approximately 150,000 square miles (388,850 square km), including the island territories of Svalbard and Jan Mayen.

ETHNIC GROUPS
Norwegian 92.7 percent; Swedish 0.7 percent; Danish 0.6 percent; Residents of former Yugoslavia 0.5 percent; Sami 0.4 percent; British 0.3 percent; other 4.8 percent (2005 estimates)

RELIGIOUS GROUPS
Lutheran Church of Norway 86 percent; Protestant 3.5 percent; Islam 2 percent; Roman Catholic 1 percent; other 7.5 percent (2005 estimates)

MAIN LANGUAGES
Norwegian (Bokmål and Nynorsk)

LITERACY
People aged 15 and above who can both read and write: 100 percent

NATIONAL HOLIDAYS
Easter (at least 5 days in March or April); Labor Day (May 1); Children's Day and Constitution Day (May 17); Midsummer's Day (June 23); All Saints' Day (November 1); Christmas Day (December 25); Boxing Day (December 26)

ROYAL FAMILY
Harald V, King of Norway (1937–), ascended the throne January 17, 1991, succeeding his father, King Olav V.
Sonja, Queen of Norway (1937–)
Haakon, Crown Prince of Norway (1973–)
Märtha Louise, Princess of Norway (1971–)

LEADERS IN POLITICS
Christian Michelsen—first prime minister of independent Norway (1905–07)
Einar Gerhardsen—prime minister 1945–51 and 1955–65; referred to as "Landsfader" (Father of the Nation)
Gro Harlem Brundtland—Norway's first female prime minister (1986–96)
Kjell Magne Bondevik—prime minister from 1997–2000 and 2001–05
Jens Stoltenberg—prime minister (2005–)

TIME LINE

IN NORWAY	IN THE WORLD
10,000 B.C. First human settlers reach Norway.	**753 B.C.** Rome is founded.
	116–17 B.C. The Roman Empire reaches its greatest extent, under Emperor Trajan (98–17).
	A.D. 600 Height of Mayan civilization
a.d. 770 Viking Age begins.	
900 Norway is united into one kingdom.	
995 Christianity is introduced into Norway.	**1000** The Chinese perfect gunpowder and begin to use it in warfare.
1217 Haakon IV becomes king.	
1349 The Black Death kills two-thirds of the population.	
1387 Norwegian royal line dies out.	
1450 Norway becomes part of Denmark.	**1530** Beginning of transatlantic slave trade organized by the Portuguese in Africa.
	1558–1603 Reign of Elizabeth I of England
	1620 Pilgrims sail the *Mayflower* to America.
	1776 U.S. Declaration of Independence
	1789–99 The French Revolution
1814 Union with Denmark ends. New union with Sweden begins.	**1861** The U.S. Civil War begins.
	1869 The Suez Canal is opened.
1884 Parliamentary system is established.	**1914** World War I begins.

IN NORWAY	IN THE WORLD
1905 Sweden recognizes independent Kingdom of Norway. Danish Prince Carl is elected king.	
1913 Norwegian women gain the right to vote.	
	1939 World War II begins.
1940 Norway is invaded and occupied by Germany. Prime Minister Johan Nygaardsvold leads the government in exile (1940–45).	
1945 Norway joins the United Nations.	**1945** The United States drops atomic bombs on Hiroshima and Nagasaki.
1949 Norway becomes a member of NATO.	**1949** The North Atlantic Treaty Organization (NATO) is formed.
	1957 The Russians launch Sputnik.
1968 Norway discovers oil in the North Sea.	**1966–69** The Chinese Cultural Revolution
1972 Norwegians vote not to join the European Union.	
1981 Norway's first female prime minister is elected.	**1986** Nuclear power disaster at Chernobyl in Ukraine
1991 King Olav V dies, King Harald V ascends the throne.	**1991** Breakup of the Soviet Union
1993 Norway resumes commercial whaling despite international moratorium.	
1994 Second vote against joining the European Union.	**1997** Hong Kong is returned to China.
2001–05 Norway is ranked top in UN Human Development Index.	**2001** Terrorists crash planes in New York, Washington, D.C., and Pennsylvania.
	2003 War in Iraq

GLOSSARY

ætt (eht)
Group of eight letters in the 24-rune alphabet.

allmannsretten (AWL-leh-mawns-reht-ten)
Every man's right to public access of the countryside.

barnehage (BAR-neh-HAH-guh)
Kindergarten for children age 4 to 7.

Bokmål (BOOK-mawl)
Language developed during Norway's union with Denmark. The spoken form is different from Danish, but the written form is nearly identical to Danish.

bunad (BOO-nahd)
Embroidered national dress.

fjord (fyord)
Very deep and narrow inlet of the sea between steep cliffs.

futhark (FEW-thark)
A name for the runic alphabet created by the first six letters of the alphabet.

fylker (FEWL-ker)
Counties; there are 19 counties in Norway, including the city of Oslo.

husmorlag (HEWS-moor-lahg)
Neighborhood group of women who do projects of common interest, such as fund raising.

joik (yoy-IK)
Sami musical tradition of yodeling that imitates animal sounds. Joiks include myths, Sami history, and commentaries on persons or current events.

Klar Melding (klahr MEHL-ding)
"Clear message," a toll-free telephone hotline to the ombudsman for children to ask questions or present problems.

kommuner (koo-MEW-ner)
Rural or urban district belonging to a county; each is administered by a council.

kvinnegruppe (KVIN-nuh-GREW-puh)
Women's group formed to discuss women's issues and contemporary literature.

middag (mid-DAHG)
Main meal of the day, eaten around 4 to 6 P.M.

Nynorsk (NEE-noshk)
Language created in reaction to Danish rule, dating from the mid-1800s and combining elements from rural dialects for a more distinctly Norwegian language than Bokmål.

runes (roons)
Angular letters of an ancient alphabet, one of the earliest forms of Germanic writing.

russ (rewss)
High-school graduates celebrate their graduation wearing *russ* gowns. *Russ* describes both the costumes and the graduate.

FURTHER INFORMATION

BOOKS

Archer, Clive. *Norway Outside the European Union: Norway and European Integration from 1994 to 2004*. Philadephia, PA: Taylor and Francis, 2004.

Braun, Eric. *Norway in Pictures*. Minneapolis, MN: Lerner Publications, 2003.

Doub, Siri Lise. *Tastes and Tales of Norway*. New York: Hippocrene Books, 2001.

Roalson, Louise and Joan Liffring-Zug, Bourret. *Norwegian Touches: History, Recipes, Folk Arts*. Iowa City, IA: Penfield Press, 2003.

Robinson, Deborah. *The Sami of Northern Europe*. Minneapolis, MN: Lerner Publications, 2002.

WEB SITES

Norway—The official site in the United States. www.norway.org

Norway—Wikipedia, the free encyclopedia. www.en.wikipedia.org/wiki/Norway

Go Norway. www.gonorway.no/

Royal House of Norway. www.kongehuset.no/default.asp?lang=eng

FILMS

Norway: From the Land of Vikings. Trailwood Films & Media, 2004.

MUSIC

Folk Music from Norway. Norway Music, 1996.

Norwegian Classical Favourites. NAXOS, 2002.

BIBLIOGRAPHY

Charbonneau, Claudette and Patricia S. Lander. *The Land and People of Norway.* New York: Harper Collins Children's Books, 1993.

Holte, Elisabeth. *Living in Norway.* New York: Abbeville Press, 1994.

Lerner Publications. *Norway in Pictures.* Minneapolis, MN: Lerner Publications, 1990.

Reynolds, Jan. *Far North: Vanishing Cultures.* San Diego, CA: Harcourt Brace Jovanovich, 1992.

Vanbers, Bent. *Of Norwegian Ways.* New York: Barnes and Noble, 1992.

Zickgraf, Ralph. *Norway.* New York: Chelsea House, 1990.

Aftenposten News from Norway. www.aftenposten.no/english/

Central Intelligence Agency World Factbook (select Norway from country list). www.cia.gov/cia/publications/factbook

The Official Norwegian Trade Portal. www.nortrade.com

Odin—Information from the government and the ministries. http:// odin.dep.no/odin/english

State of the Environment in Norway. www.environment.no/

Statistics Norway. www.ssb.no/english/

INDEX

Æthelred, King, 86
Aasen, Ivar, 93
agriculture, 10, 11, 13, 19, 50, 51, 67
Akershus Fortress, 31
allemannsretten, 63
Antarctic, 7, 16
Antarctic Treaty, 16
aquavit, 124, 129
architecture, 11, 27, 104
Arctic Circle, 15, 16, 19, 21, 48, 60, 107, 120
Arctic Ocean, 7, 114
artists

Dahl, Johan Christian, 98
  Munch, Edvard, 98 , 98, 9 ,127
  Vigeland, Gustav, 97, 127
Ascension Day, 117
Asia, 66, 70, 115
assemblies, 23, 27, 30, 87, 120

Baltic Sea, 65
baptism, 76, 77, 84, 87, 128
Berg, Eva, 43
borettslag, 80
Bouvet Island, 7, 16
Brundtland, Gro Harlem, 42, 43, 44

cabinet, 32, 33, 40, 41, 42, 68
Canute II, 29
Carl, Prince, 32, 37, 39
Carlsen, Bjørn, 111
Charles XIII, 31
cheeses, 20, 51, 123, 124, 125, 126
children, 15, 27, 42, 57, 69, 70, 73, 74, 75, 76, 78, 79, 80, 108, 111, 117, 118, 124
chocolate, 126, 127
Christianity, 28, 29, 78, 86, 87, 88, 104
Christmas, 114, 117, 121, 125
cities

Bergen, 14, 18, 23, 49, 63, 71, 73, 79, 87, 102, 117
Elverum, 33
Hedmark, 51
Longyearbyen, 16
Oppland, 51
Oslo, 11, 14, 18, 19, 21, 31, 33, 37, 40, 41, 49, 50, 55, 69, 71, 79, 81, 97, 98, 102, 108, 109, 110, 117, 118, 119, 127
Slagen, 49
Stavanger, 10, 19, 49, 69, 71, 79, 102
Svalbard, 7, 16, 24, 60, 69, 113
Tromsø, 15, 19, 33, 55, 79
Trøndelag, 10, 13, 19, 23, 50, 51, 52, 67, 86, 129
Vadsø, 65, 133
climate, 14, 21, 50, 57, 58, 60, 62, 107, 128
clothing, 105, 117
composers
    Grieg, Edvard, 99
    Nordheim, Arne, 99
confirmation, 77
conservation, 38, 57, 60, 61
constitution, 31, 32, 38, 40, 83, 118
Constitution Day, 117, 118
Cultural Heritage Act, 63

Denmark, 11, 24, 28, 29, 30, 31, 32, 33, 37, 39, 45, 47, 49, 55, 70, 84, 87, 92, 118
Dronning Maud Land, 7, 16

Easter, 117, 120, 121
education, 18, 43, 74, 78, 79
Einarson, Oddvar, 103
England, 24, 25, 28, 29, 30, 39, 86, 88, 138
environmental issues, 57, 111
Equal Status Act, 27, 43, 68
Erichsen, Bente, 103
Erik Bloodaxe, 28, 86
Europe, 8, 13, 18, 24, 27, 33, 34, 43, 49, 62, 70, 84, 85, 86, 88, 103, 104, 117, 120, 129
European Union, 45, 51
explorers
    Amundsen, Roald, 16, 112, 113, 114, 115, 127
    Arnesen, Liv, 112, 114
    Heyerdahl, Thor, 112, 115, 117

Nansen, Fridtjof, 16, 44, 70, 112, 113, 114, 115
    Sverdrup, Otto, 112, 113
    Thorseth, Ragnar, 112
exports, 50, 51, 127

Faeroe Islands, 24, 31
fauna, 20, 21
Finland, 23, 43, 45, 66, 95
Finnmark, 23, 65, 66, 95
Finns, 65, 91
fishing, 17, 18, 23, 52, 63, 66, 67, 68, 81, 107, 110
fjell, 9
fjords, 9, 10, 13, 14, 16, 23, 52, 53, 54, 55, 62, 65, 91, 108
flora, 20, 21
forestry, 11, 51
France, 29, 31, 87, 108, 127
Frcia, 126, 127
fylker, 40

gas, 48, 49, 57
Gaup, Nils, 103
Germany, 18, 33, 34, 35, 47, 70, 91, 98, 101
glaciers, 7, 8, 16, 62, 107
gods, Norse, 85
    Frey, 85
    Odin, 49, 85
    Thor, 85, 94, 112, 115, 117
Greece, 53, 111
Greenland, 24, 29, 31, 60, 87, 112
Grieg, Nordahl, 13, 102, 118

Haakon I, 28
Haakon IV, 29
Haakon V (Magnus Lagabøte), 30, 31
Haakon VI, 30, 32, 37
Haakon VII, 32, 33, 35, 37, 39, 114
Harald, Crown Prince, 39
Harald Fairhair, 28, 86
Harald III, King, 18
Harald V, 38, 137, 139
health care, 74
Henie, Sonja, 108, 109
housing, 35, 74, 80, 81
hunting, 23, 52, 54, 63, 67
hydroelectric power, 35, 47, 49, 50

Ibsen, Henrik, 93, 99, 101, 102, 117
Ice Age, 8
Iceland, 24, 29, 31, 45, 100, 112

independence, 28, 30, 31, 32, 37, 41, 118, 120
industry, 18, 47, 49, 50, 52, 53, 60, 69, 81, 103
Ireland, 24, 25, 69

Jæren Dalane, 10
Jan Mayen Island, 16
Japan, 47, 101
Jews, 34
joik, 105
Jotunheimen, 8, 62, 107
judiciary, 30

Kalmar Union, 30, 84
Kautokeino, 67, 89
Kolstad, Eva, 43
Kristiansand, 11
kvinnegruppe, 77

Labor Day, 117
lakes, 7, 23, 58, 61
Langfjellene, 10, 11
languages
    Bokmål, 91, 92, 93
    Danish, 91
    Dutch, 91
    English, 91
    Faeroese, 91
    Finnish, 65, 66, 91, 95, 125
    Frisian, 91
    German, 91
    Hungarian, 95
    Icelandic, 91
    Nynorsk, 91, 92, 93
    Riksmål, 93
    Samnorsk, 92, 93
    Swedish, 91
Lappland, 105
laws, 23, 27, 29, 30, 40, 41, 43, 63, 74, 76, 84, 127
League of Nations, 44, 70, 112
Lie, Trygve, 44, 48
life expectancy, 75
Lillehammer, 101, 108, 109
Lofoten Islands, 13, 17
Lofoten Wall, 17 (See also Lofoten islands)
Luther, Martin, 83
Lutheran Church, 76, 77, 83, 89

Magnus I, 29
Magnus VII, 30

maps
    cultural Norway, 136
    economic Norway, 134
    map of Norway, 132
Margrete, Queen, 30
Märtha, Crown Princess, 39
Märtha Louise, Princess, 38
Maud, Queen, 32, 39
Midsummer's Day, 15, 117, 120, 121
migration, 67
mining, 12, 16, 63, 67
monarchy, 32, 37, 39
mountains, 7, 8, 9, 10, 13, 14, 16, 17, 18,
    19, 23, 54, 62, 63, 81, 91, 117, 120,
    126
    Langfjellene, 10, 11
    Reka, 8
    Romsdal, 7, 8, 52
museums
    Dried Fish Museum, 17
    Norwegian Fishing Village
        Museum, 17
    Vigeland Museum, 97

Nazism, 33, 34, 118
newspapers, 15, 34, 67, 69, 92, 111
Nidaros Cathedral, 19, 83
Nobel Peace Prize, 40, 41, 70, 117
Nord-Norge, 10, 13
Nordic Council, 44, 45
Norheim, Sondre, 107, 108
North Atlantic Treaty Organization, 35
North Pole, 16, 20, 112, 113, 114
Norwegian Institute of Technology, 19

Olav I (Tryggvason), 19, 28, 29, 86, 87
Olav II (Haraldsson), 28, 29, 87, 88
Olav III, 18
Olav V, 37, 38, 137, 139
ombudsman, 42, 79, 140
Oslofjord, 11, 12, 18, 26, 33, 51, 87
Østlandet, 10, 12, 13
Outdoor Recreation Act, 63

parliament, 31, 33, 37, 40, 41, 66, 73,
    (See also Storting)
Peter I Island, 7, 16
political parties
    Center Party, 44
    Christian Democrats, 44
    Conservatives, 44
    Labor Party, 44
    Liberal Party, 43, 44

pollution, 57, 58, 59, 60, 61, 67, 111
population, 11, 16, 18, 20, 24, 30, 32,
    34, 39, 40, 49, 53, 65, 70, 93
Protestant Reformation, 83

Quisling, Vidkun, 33, 35

recipes
    kjøttkaker, 130
    strawberry cake roll, 131
recycling, 59
refugees, 34, 38, 69, 70, 71
reindeer, 20, 66, 67, 105, 125
religions
    Buddhism, 89
    Christianity, 28, 29, 44, 77, 83, 86,
        88, 98, 104, 117, 120
    Hinduism, 89
    Islam, 89
    Judaism, 89
    Pentecostal, 89
    Roman Catholic, 89
research, 8, 16, 18, 19, 45, 61, 67, 69,
    113, 115
Roestad, Bente, 111
Rogstad, Anna, 43, 68
runes, 94
russ, 117, 118, 119
Russia, 20, 23, 24, 48, 70, 86, 87, 88

sagas, 27, 86, 101
Sami, 63, 65, 66, 67, 88, 89, 91, 95, 103,
    105, 120, 125
Samiland, 105
Scotland, 24, 25, 30, 35
shipping, 18, 53, 57
skiing, 19, 37, 38, 107, 108, 109, 110,
    113, 114
smørgåsbord, 123
Sonja Haraldsen, Queen, 39
Sørlandet, 10, 11
Spitsbergen, 16
stave church, 63, 82, 104
stavkirker, (See also stave church)
Stordahl, Erling, 109
Storting, 37, 40, 41, 42, 43, 49, 51, 53,
    67, 68, 84 (see also parliament)
sustainable development, 45, 57
Svalbard, 16
Sweden, 24, 28, 29, 30, 31, 32, 35, 37,
    39, 41, 45, 47, 55, 66, 70, 84, 95, 101
Switzerland, 20

taxes, 40, 43, 57, 59, 62, 73, 74

technology, 19, 47
Telemark, 35, 107, 108, 110
theater, 67, 101, 102, 103, 117
trade, 12, 18, 24, 27, 35, 45, 47, 65,
    86, 112
transportation, 54, 58, 108
    railway, 54
Treaty of Kiel, 31
Troms, 15, 65
Trøndelag, 10
Trondheim, 12, 18, 19, 21, 79, 83, 87,
    88, 102

unemployment, 74
United Kingdom, 21
United Nations, 38, 44, 45, 57, 60, 71,
    115, 139
United States, 33, 35, 47, 69, 89, 100,
    101, 103, 108, 118
universities, 18, 79

Valhalla, 49, 85
valleys, 11, 21, 62, 115
Vestlandet, 10, 13, 18
vidder, 9,
Vigeland Park, 97, 136
Vikings, 18, 19, 24, 25, 26, 27, 63, 85,
    86, 87, 88, 94, 97, 98, 100, 104, 112,
    120, 121, 126, 128
vote, 32, 40, 41, 43, 45, 68, 79

wars
    Battle of Hafrsfjord, 28
    Battle of Stiklestad, 29, 88
    Battle of Svold, 87
    Battle of Svolder, 28
    Napoleonic Wars, 31
    World War I, 33, 69, 70, 138
    World War II, 32, , 33, 35, 39, 44,
        47, 118
welfare, 45, 68, 74
women, 27, 32, 38, 42, 43, 45, 66, 68,
    69, 75, 76, 77, 84, 85, 98, , 100, 101,
    103, 109
Worker's Protection Act, 73
workers, 70, 73, 74, 117
Working Environment Act, 47
World Wildlife Fund, 38, 61
writers
    Collett, Camilla, 100
    Hamsun, Knut, 100
    Skram, Amalie, 100
    Wergeland, Henrik, 100